Return to Deutschland

*A Canadian family searches for and finds their
German roots some 292 years back in time*

A TRUE STORY

To Dave & Ruby

[signature]

Return to Deutschland

Don Karl Dulmage

Epic
Press

Belleville, Ontario, Canada

Return to Deutschland
Copyright © 2004, Don Karl Dulmage

Library and Archives Canada Cataloguing in Publication

Dulmage, Don, 1950-

    Return to Deutschland : a Canadian family searches for and finds
their German roots some 292 years back in time / Don Karl Dulmage.

ISBN 1-55306-824-6

    1. Dolmetsch, Johann Adam--Family. 2. Dolmetsch family.
3. Germany--Genealogy. I. Title.

CS89.D83 2004
929'.2'0943   C2004-904497-4

For more information or
to order additional copies, please contact:

Don Dulmage
R.R. 1 Belleville ON
K8N 4Z1 Canada

Epic Press is an imprint of *Essence Publishing*.
For more information, contact:
20 Hanna Court, Belleville, Ontario, Canada K8P 5J2.
Phone: 1-800-238-6376 • Fax: (613) 962-3055.
E-mail: publishing@essencegroup.com
Internet: www.essencegroup.com

Preface

What if you could trace your family tree back through time? Not just a hundred years but several hundred years. What would other family members who had stayed in the country your family came from be like? Would there be any similarities between you and them, or would the traits have been lost in the gene pool and no resemblances found? And if you could find such people, would you like them and would they like you? Would you feel like family or strangers? If you have ever wondered, then this book is for you. Through the providence of Almighty God the author was afforded exactly such a journey and a peek into his family's past, as well as a visit with its present-day members. What he found changed him permanently and somehow settled his "centre of being."

Come along on this journey, which begins with the last day on earth of his ancestral father Johann Adam Dolmetsch. Born in Germany and immigrated to Ireland in 1709, Johann Adam Dolmetsch is the ancestral father of all peoples spelling their name *Dolmage*, *Dulmage*, *Delmage* or *Delmege*.

The author begins with a reasonable account of what he believes his ancestor's last day was like. Although drawn from historical fact, it is by necessity a fictionalized account. Next we find ourselves in Prince Edward County, Canada, on the shore of Lake Ontario, as the author's Canadian ancestor reflects back on that same day his great-grandfather died. While also based on historical fact, this is a fictionalized account as well. These two chapters were written using knowledge of family traits and conditions as well as attitudes and have a reasonable possibility of being very close to the truth. From there on (beginning in chapter 3) it is accurate and factual and includes photos taken along the way. This book was written to help you, the reader, share the excitement and discovery and to encourage any of you who might be so inclined to search back through your family tree as well and to help point the way.

—*Donald Karl Dulmage*
Ameliasburgh, Ontario, Canada
January 22, 2002

The History of Johannes Adam Dolmetsch

Johannes Adam Dolmetsch was born in Wurttemburg in 1678. He is believed by some to be the son of Joseph Dolmetsch and was born in Sulz. Joseph's records are incomplete except for the birthdates.

Johannes Adam is found in his younger days living in Freimersheim and was a husbandman and vine-dresser. The births of his first two sons are recorded in the church in Alzey and other children are recorded in the church in Freimersheim. His first wife Anna died while he lived there and he remarried a few months later to Elisabeth. She also bore him children. In 1709 we find him in Pforzheim getting ready to leave Germany in the mass migration of 1709. He went down the rivers with others from that area by flat-bottomed boats and next appears in Rotterdam. It is said he helped organize the migration of some 3000 people who were leaving Germany at that time. He is listed as a passenger with his family on the ship, Batchelor and arrived in Blackheath, England where he registered at the refugee camp there. Records show he was thirty years old. With many of his countrymen, some of whom were neighbours and relatives, he went to Rathkeale, Ireland where they settled on the Lord Southwell Estate. Very soon they had a small village built similarly to what they would have had in Germany. It was known as Court Matrix. There is a lot of verifiable history readily available on this place. Several books have been written that include many references to the Dolmetsch family. Johann Adam Dolmetsch died at Castle Matrix in 1751. His oldest son Gerhardt who was born in Germany and migrated with him carried on at Court Matrix. The Dolmetsch family and their neighbours, the Hacks, the Imbergers, the Dedlors, the Hoffmans, the Muellers, the Lorentzs and the Schweitzers, prospered in Ireland and many references tell of their ability to farm profitably as well as some successful ventures in the linen-making trade. Around this time, probably out of sheer necessity, the spellings of many of these German names were Anglicized. Dolmetsch became Dolmage (mentioned in Stammfolge der Familie Dolmetsch), Imberger became Embury, Schwietzer became Switzer, Mueller became Miller, Hack became Heck, Dedlor became Detlor, Lorentz became Lawrence and Hoffman became Huffman. Jacob Dolmage was the first Dolmetsch generation to use the "Dolmage" spelling. Jacob's sons used the spelling Dulmage. That spelling can be found throughout Canada as well as the USA and it is reasonably safe to say all Dulmage families can trace their ancestry to Johannes Adam Dolmetsch with little difficulty. The members of the family who stayed in Ireland often use the spelling Delmage but they are, as well, direct descendants of our Johannes Adam Dolmetsch. It is amazing to realize the impact his life had down through the ages. As the Dolmages and their friends prospered in Ireland they were burdened with more and more taxes. As with all Dolmetsches there came a moment when enough was enough. In 1760 Jacob Dolmage and his family left Ireland for the American colonies. The ship they came on was the Pery. They arrived in the area of present day New York and after a while secured property on Duane's Patent in the Mohawk Valley near Camden, New York (on the New York/Vermont border). Evidence of their stay still exists and although the Dolmage homes are destroyed a few of their neighbours' and relatives' houses still remain to this day.

Jacob Dolmage's sons were John, Jacob Jr. and David. During the American Revolution the Dulmage boys sided with the British Crown out of respect and thankfulness for the help their family had received in England and Ireland when times were hard. Many of their neighbours who had moved with them to Ireland and now America did the same. When the British Crown was ousted from the American Colonies John and David Dulmage headed north to what is now Canada where they received land grants for their military services. Jacob Jr. stayed behind and some American Dulmages (but not all) may trace their line to him. Their father, Jacob Dolmage died near Albany, New York in 1781. John Dulmage settled near the present day town of Prescott, Ontario and many Dulmages can be found there even today.

David settled in Prince Edward County, Ontario, which is about the centre of the north shore of Lake Ontario and is almost an island hanging out into the lake. Many of his descendants still live there including the author of this article, Donald Karl Dulmage. While time and distance have separated the various lines of der familie Dolmetsch we still share some common ancestry and it is my hope we can at least be good friends.

—Ameliasburgh, Ontario, Canada July 2000
Donald Karl Dulmage

Chapter 1

Reflections

The warm sun felt good against his shirt. It was one of the first real, sunny, warm days he had seen in quite a while. As Johann Adam made his way along the fence to the workshop behind his house he felt more tired than usual. His left foot felt a bit funny, sort of like it was wet, but stiff as well. His side hurt as he sat down on a barrel to look over the view. He remembered how his Uncle Zacharius, back in Deutschland, always used to push in on his left side. Adam wondered if he had inherited some physical problem from his family. He could remember his aunt telling his uncle, "Not pushing on your side Zach!" "Actually," he thought, "that is how she would have said it but it would have been in Deutsch." It seemed strange now to think about it. It seemed so long ago. He now found himself thinking more and more in English. "How can that be?" he thought. "I was born in Deutschland and raised the better part of my family there." It seemed strange to think in English. "After all," he thought, "I often speak the old language. It is not lost. It is only that to be living here and for making money English is necessary." Ireland had been good to him. He had done well here, and so had his sons, but now, today, he missed the homeland. He thought back to the time he had learned to speak English. Anna had known it. He never knew why and didn't take the time to ask. After all, who would have thought that she would have died so young. "She was a good woman," he thought. He had learned a lot from her. He remembered how she taught him to say his "Ws" by blowing out the candles. Life was fun back then, but then the raids came. Still, if things had been different, he might have stayed. Maybe if Anna had lived, he would have. He missed his friends. There was the widow Neuschwander from Alzey. They had been to her place for dinner many times. She lived a simpler life than he desired, still, Anna had liked her a lot and even now, he could remember her good desserts. He had heard that her family had also left. They had gone straight to the Americas. He had often heard his grandson, Jacob, talk about going there as well. "He is a lot like I was," he thought. "Not like his father, Gerhardt, my oldest son, who is quite content to stay here in Ireland." He thought about the family. He was glad when the Wesley brothers had come to Court Matrix. Things were a little bit too free here for the younger ones and with no Lutheran church to keep them on track he had been worried about them. "Anna would have looked after that too," he thought. "She knew her Bible." Still, he was glad the children seemed to be carrying on strong Christian beliefs. He thought about Elisabeth who had just made his dinner. She was a good woman as well, but it was somehow different. She had been a younger friend of Anna's and had been a big help after Anna died. "She is a good cook," he thought. "I probably took the easy path out when I married her but what is a man supposed to do with three small children and no mother to look after them." It had worked out okay and while he cared for her very much, it was, still, somehow different. His foot began to go to sleep and he changed his position to alleviate the problem. He could see his son Gerhardt and his grandson Jacob coming up the lane from the pasture. There were now four generations of the family living here. He guessed that was more of a privilege than anyone could ask for. "Jacob looks more like my father everyday," he thought. He sighed. It had been a long time since he had thought about his father. As he mulled it over in his mind, he could almost smell the leather in his father's old shop in Sulz. "I liked my father," he thought, "but I just could not get along with him." He remembered the day he had left. They had had a big argument that had ended with him packing his rucksack and walking out. "Dad never gave me credit for having any brains," he thought. He remembered the discussion his father had had with the officials over registering the family birth records at the local church. "As long as that idiot is there," Joseph had said, "There will be no Dolmetsches registered there from this household!" He had offered to fill out the information for his father, but had been cut down with sharp stinging words. "I wonder if Poppa couldn't read?" he thought, but dismissed that quickly. He had been far too good with money and business. That was not a possibility. "It doesn't matter anymore," he thought. " Poppa is long gone by now. He was forty years old when I was born and I am now seventy-three so he is either dead and buried or the oldest living man and I think the latter is impossible." He wondered what it would have been like if he had stayed in Sulz. If only he and his father could have gotten along better. It had been warmer there, but then, there was no Anna. He had met her in Alzey, in the market square, that same week he had left home. There it was again. His thoughts of Anna. She had been an important part of his life and even now some fifty years after her death she still influenced him. "Family, that is important," he thought. He had tried to keep from speaking to the boys after they reached that stage of life where you could see that strong light in their eyes. He had slipped up a few times in the typical Dolmetsch way, but still, he had tried to behave for the most part. He remembered, all too well, the sting of his father's criticism and was determined to spare his sons that same displeasure. It had turned out well, too. All his children seemed to have their feet under them. They had not been a great source of worry since coming here. Still, he wished they had not changed their name. Gerhardt had explained to him repeatedly that the Irish just couldn't figure out how to pronounce "Dolmetsch." "That was the truth," he thought. He had just this past week been called "Mr. Doolmittesh." What was wrong with these people? Couldn't they say it the way it was spelled? "The English speaking people use only half of the alphabet," he had told Gerhardt. "If they would pronounce every letter as we do in Deutsch there would be no problem!" Still, it bothered him. Dolmage didn't seem quite right either. When Jacob changed his sons' last name to

Dulmage that was the final straw for Johann Adam. "What if someone from Uncle Zach's or Uncle Ludwig's came looking for the family," he had said. "Why, they wouldn't be able to find their own cousins." As he thought about it he decided to add it to his morning prayer. It was getting hot now and so he rolled up his sleeves. His left elbow stung a bit in the hot sun but he didn't care. It had done that for about twenty years and so he figured if it was anything serious it would have killed him long ago.

He glanced out over the field once more and then closed his eyes. "Almighty God," he prayed, "today I am thanking You for Your goodness to me. I have not forgotten how You took care of me in the homeland and led me here. Many thanks for my family and the joy they have brought me. Many thanks for guiding me. I don't know why You do, because both You and I know how I really am, but I thank You anyway. I am also thanking You for your Son, Jesus Christ who died in my place for my many sins. Dear God, today I am thinking of the homeland and the ones we left there. I thought, dear God, we would them again see, but I realize now it will not be this side of heaven. I ask, dear God, that You will someday 'der Familie Dolmetsch' reunite wherever they may be. I know this is a big request but as You told Moses in the desert, You are 'the God of the impossible' so, I ask You to hear my bidding. Thank You for a long and interesting life. Bis spaeter, (till later). Johann Adam Dolmetsch."

He liked to sign his prayers that way and he was sure God didn't mind. He kept his eyes closed and eventually drifted off to sleep.

Later that afternoon young David Dulmage came running home from school. If he could get into the workshop and grab his cane, maybe he could try climbing the big hill again that he had found the previous year. If his mother saw him first there would be chores to do, after, of course, that horrible thing all school boys had to deal with, changing out of their school clothes. As he rounded the corner by the back gate he saw his great-grandfather lying strangely on the floor by their favourite window. He ran to him. "Tick-tack-Poppa," he cried, "wake up!" He reached out and shook the old man's shoulder. It seemed cold and stiff. He ran out of the workshop and around to the barn where he saw his father Jacob working in the doorway. "Poppa, come quick!" he shouted. "Something is wrong with Urgrossvater!" (Great-grandfather).

Jacob dropped the hoe he was sharpening and came running to the workshop. His own father, Gerhardt, had also heard David's cry for help and came following along behind. When Jacob saw his grandfather, Johann Adam, he paled noticeably. He knew instantly what was wrong. He straightened the old man's legs and spoke softly in Deutsch to his young son. In the old family language, with a hoarse voice, he explained to the young boy that Urgrossvater was dead. He was now in heaven just like the Brother Wesley had said. With his young grandson, David, clinging to his shoulder and with tears welling up in his eyes old Gerhardt knelt down beside his son Jacob and grandson David and spoke to the body of his aged father. "Du war ein gutes Vater. Vati, Ich bin stolz das Ich dein Sohn war."(You were a great father, Dad. I am proud to have been your son.) As he stood up he switched back into English. "Come, Jacob, David. We had better go tell the women folk."

Chapter 2

Canada

David looked out the window toward Port Milford. He thought back to the time in Ireland when he had found his great-grandfather, Johann Adam Dolmetsch lying dead in the afternoon sun. "He must have been quite a man," he thought. "Leaving all he knew in Germany to start a new life. Sailing up the Rhine to Rotterdam, Holland, then to England and on to Ireland. I wonder what that must have been like, to leave the land you were born in and all your relatives and strike out for the unknown." It did not occur to David that he, himself, had a similar experience. He had admired his great-grandfather. A strong, tall man with a determination and a calmness about him that seemed to say, "don't worry, this will all work out."

Grandpa Gerhardt was strong too, but in a different way. He had noticed how the two men respected each other but still kept their distance. He could still hear their thick German accents when they spoke. He sometimes found himself thinking in German even though he had never really learned to speak it very well. As he looked out on the port at the mirrored water it was there again. "Ruhig," (Calm, still) came to his mind. "It must be something in the blood," he thought. He wondered how his brother John was making out at Prescott. They had hoped to have land grants together, but it had not worked out. Now they were separated by several days travel. It had been a few months now since he had heard from John. "And then," he thought, "there is Jake." His other brother had gone south to New Jersey in search of his fortune and had never been heard from again. When the Revolution broke out with the American Colonists he was already gone, although he had heard reports that Jacob had been seen with one of the British units. David and John had taken up arms on the British side. After all, they were born in Ireland so whom else would they side with. "The British have been very good to my family," he thought. "What else were we supposed to do" No one could have predicted they would have lost that war but they did. It did not matter to David or John as they chose their stand as a matter of principle, regardless of what lay ahead. "I know Great-Grandfather would have approved," he thought. "Now, Grandpa Gerhardt might have thought differently." Their own father, Jacob Dolmage, had not wanted to get involved. "I'm too old for this fighting stuff," he had said. "I brought you boys here and I guess from now on you will have to carry on, on your own. Your mother and I are going to go back to New York where it is a bit safer. The governor has given us permission to live there." Somehow it didn't seem right but the boys knew better than to argue. Too much discussion with their father Jacob would always bring the same result. He would bang his cane on the floor and then push his tall, lanky body to his feet. "Stille!" (quiet) he would shout in the old German. David smiled as he thought about it. "And 'Stille' we would be too," he remembered.

A lot had happened since his great-grandfather had left Germany. Old Johann Adam had talked about the family there often. Uncle Ludwig and Uncle Zach were the subject of many dinner conversations. He had rarely talked about his own father though. "I wonder what went wrong there?" David thought. His great-grandfather had started once to tell him a bit about it but someone had come along just then and he had never approached the subject again. "I wonder if we will ever see any of them," David thought. "Certainly, it seems impossible now, but things can change. Maybe some of them will come to Canada someday. And what about my family in Ireland? I wonder what has happened to them. I guess we could have stayed but Dad had had about all of young Southwell's nonsense he could stand. With John already in America he needed little encouragement to leave. Now here I am, born in Ireland to German immigrants, moved to New York in America, till the trouble started, lost everything I had worked for in the Revolution and I am now starting over at an age when I should have been beginning to prosper. I seem to find no end of trouble."

"Still," he thought, as he turned back to the window for one last look before going to bed, "there is something about this place, this Prince Edward County, that feels just right." For some reason that he did not fully understand, he seemed for the first time in his life to be truly at home. It seemed like a good place to raise a family and quite a family he had too. It was now up to ten children and he loved every one of them. Mary had asked if they could name the last boy, (born on their stopover in Sorel) David. He had resisted using his own name but with ten children soon one began running out of options. "He has those same squinting eyes like yours dear," she had said. "Like mine," he thought, "she hadn't known the family in Ireland but folks around Rathkeale could tell by those eyes that we were all from the same family. Even though not all the children had them as pronounced as his (and now young David's) there was still, as Great-Grandfather would say 'ein stark familie (a strong family) resemblance.'" He loved the way Great-Grandfather murdered the English language. If the German was close he simply used it and fitted the new English words in wherever they seemed to be needed. No one had ever questioned him on it. They wouldn't dare. To upset Johann Adam Dolmetsch was about the same as teasing an old bull. You might get away with it for a while, but not forever. David could still remember how quiet it got at the cattle sale when that man had made fun of Great-Grandfather once too often. "I'm not like that," David thought. "I can hold my own, to be sure, but Great-Grandfather, or 'old J.A.' (as the locals called him) knew how to command respect. I wonder what will happen to this family in the years to come?" he thought. With that he blew out the lamp and went up to bed.

Chapter 3

Return to Germany

on Dulmage stared out the window as the plane bumped along the pavement on its way to the runway. It was May 27, 2000, the turn of the century. His wife, Linda, had asked if they could go to Germany to see the Passion Play in Oberammergau. Linda had said that it had, for a long time, been a goal of hers to see the Passion Play at the beginning of the new millennium. Don had always wanted to go to Germany and this was a good excuse. While he had no disagreement with the Bible or the life of Christ and the telling of the story he had no interest in drama presentations per se. Still the chance to visit the land of his ancestor, Johann Adam Dolmetsch, greatly interested him. "One could tolerate almost anything for a day," he thought, so he agreed to go. "I want to spend at least some time in Pforzheim," he had said. Pforzheim was the last place his ancestor Johann Adam Dolmetsch had been officially recorded as being in before he left Germany for Ireland by way of Rotterdam and England in 1709.

He had wondered about learning German but people had told them everyone in Europe speaks English, so he hadn't worried about it. In his suitcase were a lot of papers with the names of places the family had lived along with a hand written summary of the details. Some of the information he had gleaned from his own research and some had come from Reta Selleck in North Carolina. Also a descendant of David Dulmage, Reta had been a great help in providing information at exactly the right moment in his life. Despite the fact that he didn't particularly enjoy flying he was now getting anxious to get there. The flight was long and uneventful. Don felt cramped in his window seat as he peered out for a glimpse of the land of his forefathers. It was foggy as they flew in from the Atlantic coast and other than the occasional opening through the thick clouds he had seen nothing. Now the fog began clearing and some green patches of land could be seen down below. The plane banked sharply and began to descend. The ground and some sort of a river could now be seen. It looked just like home which surprised him. Why that did he didn't really know. Soon they were on the ground and walking through the Airport. "There does not seem to be a lot of English being spoken here," he thought as he waited his turn to show their passports and check their luggage. In a matter of minutes they were done and on their way through the terminal to find the train for Pforzheim. It was no small task. Although they had a German rail-pass, they had no idea what they were looking for. The lack of German was already a handicap and they had been here less than an hour. "Too late now," he thought, "we will just have to make the best of it." Finally he saw a desk in the main hallway with a DB rail sign on it. The man, although not fluent in English, was able to direct them to the platform. The young lady at the ticket counter understood what he needed to know and printed out a route advisory. She then showed them where to catch the train. After about twenty minutes the train pulled up. Karlsruhe was the first stop. From there they had to switch trains for Pforzheim. It seemed very confusing at first but after asking five or six people they finally found their train. It was beginning to make sense. As they sat in the compartment waiting to leave, the conductor came running through shouting something in German. A security man followed him and motioned Don to get up. "What?" Don asked. The Guard seemed to realize Don did not understand and began to repeat slowly, "Bomb in die Bahnhof, bomb in die Bahnhof, yes? You go!" Quickly they exited the train and followed the people out of the station into the parking lot. After about twenty minutes a security guard came out and blew his whistle. "Alles okay" he said and motioned them back inside.

They were barely seated when the train began to move. Soon they were out of the city and crossing the German countryside to the place called Pforzheim. By now the long day had started to affect them. They had been awake more or less for over twenty-four hours. Soon, however, the train began slowing and Don saw the sign "Pfozheim" flash by the window. Within minutes they were in the station and dragging their suitcases off of the train. Years of travel in North America had taught them to travel light so they now had only one medium-sized suitcase each. Despite being extremely tired they stopped under the Pforzheim sign on the platform and Linda snapped a picture of Don. As they walked outside the Bahnhof (train station) Don realized he was now walking on ground that he could be certain Johann Adam Dolmetsch had walked on some 291 years before. Strangely, it felt right. It was almost as if the soil knew he should be here. He thought about how strange it would sound to try and explain that to someone who had never experienced it. Finally he decided that didn't matter. He was here and he intended to fully enjoy the experience. Pforzheim was a beautiful city. Built on a hill, most of the streets run up hill or down. At the bottom of the hill several small rivers meet. There was a mixture of the old and the new but for some reason they never seemed to clash. As they left the Bahnhof Don found a taxi and asked him to take them to a "gut hotel"(good hotel). The driver loaded their suitcases and then started down the street. Soon they stopped in front of the Park Hotel. One could quickly see that it was definitely a "gut hotel." Polished brass railings were evident and stood out against the spotless, dark coloured carpets. Don went to the desk as Linda stood to the side. "Ein zimmer bitte" he stammered. "Doppel?" the desk clerk asked. "Ja," said Don relieved to be able to get by on so little German. Immediately the desk clerk switched to English and the transaction was completed. They took the elevator to their room and stretched out for a short nap. After about an hour or so they woke, showered and dressed for the evening meal. The restaurant was wonderful. The meal was excellent, although it was served in stages that seemed to take a long time in between. Don guessed he was too tired to appreciate it all, but it tasted good just the same. After about an hour and a half they went for a short walk by the river and then returned to their room for a good night's sleep.

Morning seemed to come early. They slowly awoke, showered and dressed for the day. Then they went downstairs for breakfast. Breakfast, or "fruhstuck" as the German people called it, was served buffet style. While not the type of food they would normally have eaten for breakfast back home, it was nevertheless excellent food and they both enjoyed it very much. Soon they were back in their room getting ready to check out and continue their train trip. At the desk Don asked to see a phone book. The clerk offered to help. Don said he wanted to check for descendants of his ancestors. Without a moment's hesitation the clerk opened the page to D as Don tried to explain the spelling was different from the Dulmage on his credit card. "Yes sir, I know!" the clerk replied as he showed Don the names in the book. There were two of them, but they were spelled Dollmetsch. Don had read about the double 'L' spelling but was quite unprepared to find it this quickly. He wrote the names and addresses on a sheet of paper and put it in his wallet. This caught him completely off-guard and he needed time to sort through it in his mind. He could not communicate in German and he was secretly worried these Dollmetsch people would not be interested anyway. That thought would later prove to be, most likely, the truth. After a quick check, to make sure they had everything, they set out for the day. They decided to walk back uphill to the Bahnhof so as to allow themselves a chance to enjoy the city as it really was. They had to stop once to rest but soon they were back in the Bahnhof checking the schedule for the train to Speyer. There was a Pfalzer Museum there. Pfalzer was the German word for Palatine. Linda and Don both had Palatine ancestors so it seemed like a good idea to visit a museum devoted to these people and their area in Germany. Almost before they were ready the train pulled into the Bahnhof at Speyer. By now the sun was high and hot. As Don looked around he saw a young man in his thirties sitting in a Mercedes taxi. He was wearing a blue-checked flannel shirt. In fact Don had an almost exact match to it in his closet at home. Obviously this man would be a kindred spirit he thought and his judgement proved to be right on. The driver's name was Michael Spielmeyer. It was posted on his ID for all to see. Don showed him the guidebook with the Pfalzer Museum in it and Michael nodded. As they wound through the cobblestone streets they had to drive right by the bottom of a large tower-like building. Linda was fascinated by this and took a picture as they passed by. Michael smiled and drove on. Soon he pointed to the museum. Something was wrong. There were workmen on scaffolding outside and the doors were closed. "Is it open?" Don asked. Michael seemed to understand. "Eine moment," Michael said. He opened the trunk and took out their travel bags then he ran into the museum. When he reappeared, his face told the story. "Nein," he said and then pointed to the cathedral and square not far from the museum. Don caught on immediately. "We might as well see something while we are here," he thought. Speyer was one of the towns listed as being home to his Dolmetsch ancestors so he thought it was a good idea to spend some time here. He pointed to his watch and showed Michael that he wanted to be picked up right there at 3:00. Michael understood perfectly and was on his way. Don and Linda each took turns visiting the cathedral. One stayed with their bags while the other visited the gigantic building. There were several of the Kaisers buried here they discovered. They then spent time roaming the courtyard and watching a group of school children playing in front of the cathedral. Some even crawled up into the empty fountain, which made for a great picture. Time seemed to fly as they walked around the area.

True to his word, right at 3:00 Michael drove up in his taxi for the return trip to the Bahnhof. This time they drove right through the tower-like building. Michael slowed to a crawl so Linda could get a better picture. Soon they were at the train station and Don and Michael settled up for both rides. Don gave Michael a brand new Canadian toonie (two dollar coin) as a souvenir. Michael seemed pleased and asked if they were "Kanadier." "Ja," Don replied. Michael gave him a big thumbs-up sign and they parted. Although unable to speak to each other they could both tell they were similar personalities just the same.

They decided the next stop would be Worms (pronounced in German "Verms"). It seemed a longer distance to travel this time, even though it didn't look like it on the map. Don figured they must be getting tired. The Worms train station was a busy place. Don found a taxi driven by an older woman. He picked it because it was the only non-Mercedes car in the group. He asked the driver to take them to "Ein gut hotel, bitte" She looked at him and said, "Alles gut." "Nein," Don replied but was too tired to say much more. She dropped them off in front of a small hotel next to a very old church. They went up the steps and were greeted at the desk by a blond, middle-aged woman. "Ein zimmer, doppel," Don said. She replied with a barrage of questions in German. Don had already used up most of his German vocabulary and so was at a total loss to understand what she had said. He repeated himself wondering what he might have said wrong but she replied the same way as before. Soon both of them were becoming very frustrated. "Nein," she said, "full, full." Don knew perfectly well that the hotel was not full but he was just as frustrated as she was and so was glad to leave. By now he was beginning to get a bit cranky. Linda could tell by the way he walked that his patience was wearing thin. Dragging their bags on the tiny wheels, they roamed the streets. Eventually they came to the post office. Don had written some postcards to some of their friends back home. One was to the Vanderveldes who lived just a few miles from them in Ontario and the other was to Joe and Elsie Nighswander who lived in Altona, Ontario. Joe and Elsie also shared a German (and Swiss) heritage with Don. They had been friends of Don's since he was six years old and despite the fact that Joe was the same age as Don's father they had always gotten along very well together. Their friendship had been re-established a few years before when Joe and Elsie had been driving through the village of Ameliasburgh, Ontario, where Don and Linda lived. He had seen Don's name on the cattle truck in the yard and had decided to see if this was the same Don Dulmage they had known years before. They had kept in touch ever since. Don had written them while Linda and Don were in Pforzheim, as both Elsie and Joe had ancestors who also came from this general area. Don went up the steps into the post office while Linda watched their bags outside. He walked up to the counter and shoved the letters through."Luft" he said. Figuring if Lufthansa was the airline then luft should tell what he wanted. He guessed right again. The clerk told him how much and although Don did not understand he had a vague idea how much it should be and handed the clerk the appropriate bill. Again it worked perfectly and soon he was back outside. By now his feet hurt and he was hungry. Hungry was not a good state of mind for this 286-pound Canadian. Used to working hard all day, now, even though he was retired, his hunger clock was still perfectly punctual. Linda was careful as she spoke to him. She could see he was in no mood for light conversation. He had been pushing on his left rib cage all day but she had held her tongue. Since a fall in his shop some years before he had a terrible time with pain in his left side. Often he would push on it to try and make it more comfortable just as he was doing now, but somehow she sensed this was not the time or the place to reprimand him for it. She hoped they would stop for the night soon. She was desperately tired herself. They walked on looking for possible hotels. Just when Don was about to try to hail another taxi Linda spotted the Dom Hotel. It was set in one of the old store fronts that ringed the marktplatz or market square but it appeared to be a very nice place. They pushed through the door and went inside. Two young women in their late teens or early twenties were at the desk. Don asked for a room ("zimmer" and "bitte" had long since passed from his mind.) Much to his surprise both young women spoke excellent English and wasted no time in getting them a room. Don lay on the bed for what seemed a long time as his body sighed with relief. Soon they stirred and freshened up. Moments later they were on the elevator going down to the second floor restaurant. The food was excellent as was the service. Within no time Don was back to his easygoing self. After a leisurely meal they made their way back to their room and were soon fast asleep.

Morning seemed to come far too early. As Don awoke he sensed he was stiff and sore from the night before. "Too much walking for one day," he thought. Soon enough though, they were ready to meet the day. After a good breakfast they headed downstairs with their bags to the checkout. "Good morning Mr. Dulmage" the desk clerk said. "It is your 'burtsday'(combination of the German geburtstag and English birthday) today, yes?" Don had almost forgotten, but yes, it was in fact, his fiftieth birthday. "How did you know that?" he asked. "From your pass" (passport) she said. "I noticed it on the information when you checked in."

They settled their bill and decided to walk to the Bahnhof. It was, they had been told, not far away. As they walked up the hill Linda noticed a group of statues in a small park. She went to investigate. It was a memorial to the Reformer, Martin Luther and his colleagues. Even though it was not yet very bright out she took some photos to remember it by. Finally they came to the train station. Once one passed through the doors it was like entering another world. Behind them was the town they had just left with all its hustle and bustle and before them was the path to almost anywhere in Germany they wished to go. Today, the chosen destination was Alzey. That was where some of the records for Johann Adam Dolmetsch had been located and Don wanted to see the town and its churches if possible. Also he hoped to be able to visit Freimersheim but that was only an option at this point and from what he could see on the train map, no train actually went there. Even the train for Alzey was hard enough to find. Worms was a rather large station and there were just too many options. As they sat on the platform trying to figure out which train to take a group of school children were playing behind them. Linda, who was a retired schoolteacher, took an interest in this activity. One of the girls in the group sat down beside her and looked at her and smiled. Linda spoke to her in English and the girl called one of her friends over. This friend spoke perfect English. She told them she was from the USA but her family had moved here with the US military. Afterwards they had remained in Germany. Soon many of the children were walking up in front of Don and Linda. They would stop in front of them and smile then say, "Hello, how are you?" Most would then lose their composure and run off in a stifled giggle. Don and Linda both found this very enjoyable. Linda, with her school teacher training, was surprised to see the teachers did not even once venture over or ask any of the children what was going on. "I would certainly have wanted to know if I was their teacher," she thought. Moments later her thoughts were interrupted by a tall elderly German woman in a well-tailored red dress who came over and started talking to her. Linda had no idea what the woman was talking about but it was obvious she was friendly. Linda held up her hands in a gesture that is universally understood for "I don't understand." The lady barely batted an eye. Linda looked at Don for help. Although Don could not speak German he had at least enough words to convey that fact. Don tried.

"Ich bin Kanadier," he stammered. The lady smiled and pointed to an older man standing farther down the platform. "Mein mann," she said and smiled. Then she called him. At first he ignored her and looked away but then he came slowly toward them. She said something to him in German and Don repeated his "Ich bin Kanadier." "Englisch?" the man asked. And then he slowly said a couple of carefully spoken English words. "English, in school, before sixty years," he said. "Nie gesprochen" (never spoken). Don understood despite the grammar.

Having grown up near Toronto and having lived in Montreal he was used to communicating with immigrants of every persuasion and if pressed, could imitate any group you asked for. It was a terrible pastime but over the years he had found it very helpful because he could often understand people who spoke very little English just from his days of imitating their speech. Linda had no such inclinations. She, in fact, would often hand the phone to Don when someone called who had a distinctive accent. Right at this moment though his skills came in handy. Within a few minutes Don and the elderly man were carrying on a conversation. It was extremely pained and slow but somehow they were able to communicate. Don tried French. He had learned a basic type of French while working in the garage business, for a few years, in Montreal. Sure enough the elderly German nodded. He too had a working knowledge of French and so they stood there talking at a snail's pace using the words of whatever language seemed to be mutually understandable. Don asked about Alzey. He pronounced it "Allzee" but the old man immediately corrected him. "Owls-eye," he said and so "Owls-eye," it was. As it turned out the old couple were also going to Alzey and so they would show them the way. With that problem solved, the lady began showing Linda her dress. It appeared she had made it. The workmanship was excellent. Next she told them how she had fallen and showed them a large scar on her left wrist. The man explained to Don that the doctor had been little help. Instinctively from his farming days Don grasped her hand to check its temperature. (He always did this with cattle and could often tell an animal's state of health before problems escalated.) Her hands were very cold but he smiled. "We say cold hands, warm heart!" he said quoting an old adage he had often heard while growing up. The lady smiled and nodded. Little did he know at the time she had understood perfectly. The German was very close (kault hande, warm herz) and the saying was well known there as well. A few moments later the train pulled in to the Bahnhof and they boarded together. Don and Linda moved back in the car not wanting to infringe on the couple's privacy.

They were immediately reprimanded and the couple insisted that they sit with them. Don pulled out some papers he had gotten from Reta Selleck from the front of his small suitcase and showed the old man. The man understood immediately and asked about the Dulmage and Dolmetsch spelling plainly visible on the page. "Vorfar?" he asked. That sounded close to forefather to Don and he nodded. The man looked over the page. "Ah Freimersheim," he said and motioned to the window, then pointed at his watch. About ten minutes later he pointed out the window and made a motion with his hand indicating it was over the hill. "Freimersheim" he said and again pointed out the window. All the while the lady talked nonstop to Linda, who hardly understood a word although the hand motions sometimes helped. Finally the old man told his wife that she was "dumkopf als die Frau hatt kein Deutsch"(dumb-head as the woman has no German). Don understood this perfectly. She waved her husband off and kept right on talking. He told her this time "der Man hatt bischen (bit) Deutsch, (German) bischen Francosen (French) aber die Frau hatt nichts" (the man has a bit of German, a bit of French but the woman has nothing). She waved him off and said "Dumkopf"(dummy). He laughed and said "okay, Sie habt perfeckt Englisch" (okay, she has perfect English) and he laughed again. In fact they all did. The English and German were close enough they could all understand. Soon they were at the Alzey station and disembarked. The couple showed Don and Linda where they could get a taxi if they wanted but they decided to walk through the town. Alzey was very much like Pforzheim in that it was built on a hill with the train station at the top and the main part of the town below it. Don and Linda scouted around a bit till they found a church steeple sticking up in the distance and then headed for it. It was raining lightly now but that was no big problem. The church was farther than it appeared but eventually they reached the town square. They found the Evangelische Kirsche (Protestant church) and then around the corner the Katholik (Catholic) church. Don knew that he was walking on ground he could be sure that his ancestor Johann Adam Dolmetsch had walked on before. It was more than he had ever hoped for and seemed to fill a need within. They spent quite a bit of time walking around the church. Unfortunately it was closed. Then they began to roam around the town. As they walked up one street, stepping aside on the narrow streets so the cars could pass, they walked by a balcony where a man and his wife were having coffee and a morning cigarette. Seeing Don and Linda dragging their small-wheeled suitcases behind them, the man grinned and nodded. "Morgen." he said "Morgen," (morning) Don replied. "We must look silly towing our suitcases all over town," Don thought. It didn't matter much though as no one really knew who they were or would ever see them again. A little farther up the street Don saw a book on Alzey in a bookstore window. It also said historische on it so he thought it must be a history book on Alzey. Once inside it took awhile to get the clerk to understand what he wanted, as the book was in the display window and was not visible from inside of the store. Don asked for "der fenster buch" (the window book) and pointed. At first he was met with a blank stare. He wondered what he had said wrong. He had no idea so he persisted. He pointed to the window and said "fenster?" (window) "Ja," the clerk ventured cautiously. "Buch" (book) he asked. The clerk looked confused. About that time the owner stepped in to help. Don tried again. By now he was embarrassed. Gingerly he said "fenster, buch, Alzey?" " Ah ja," said the owner. "Alzey buch in fenster." "Ja!" said Don, relieved to be spared further humiliation. With that, the owner stepped around the wall into the display window and returned with the book. He looked questioningly at Don who nodded and smiled. Within minutes he had paid and they were on their way again. They decided they had seen about as much as they could for now and headed back up the hill to the Bahnhof. Once there, they checked the map at the station for Freimersheim. After a while they found it. The only problem was there was a Framersheim and a Feimersheim. Which was it? A dump truck driver came over and tried to help. He was a decent fellow and although he didn't speak English he did his best to help. A taxi was the only option and Don who was already past frustration with his book-buying escapade, decided to return to the Bahnhof to continue their journey. How he wished he knew the language better but it was too late for that now.

After a short wait they were back on the train again and heading for the city of Mainz and the Gutenberg Museum. The train ride seemed incredibly short. Don thought it must seem so because of so much going on inside his head. In actual distance it was really quite a long way. The Bahnhof in Mainz was being restored. As they walked through the station they walked around scaffolding and construction materials. Eventually they found their way to the street. Straight across from the train station was the Central Hotel. It looked like it had been there forever. They decided to give it a try. The girl at the desk, who spoke excellent English, took care of them in no time and was very helpful. After getting them a room she provided them with a walking guide of the city and directions to the Marktplatz and the Gutenberg Museum. Gutenberg, the father of the printing press had made his claim to fame by first printing the Bible. Both Don and Linda had an in-depth knowledge of this precious book so the museum was for them a "must see." The walk to the Marktplatz and the museum took a fair amount of time but it was a very interesting town and they enjoyed it all. They stopped at a vendor's cart for a hot dog. It was not like the hot dogs at home as the bun was baked right on the weiner however it tasted very good and they were soon finished eating and back on their way. The Gutenberg Museum despite its ancient subject matter was a very modern building. Don thought perhaps a bit too modern but nevertheless they spent a couple of hours there looking at the old printing displays, the early Bibles, as well as watching a dramatization (in German only) of Gutenberg's life work. Despite the language barrier the acting was so good it really didn't seem to matter.

Soon they were back outside. It was raining now as they walked toward the Rhine river. Linda had her heart set on a Rhine cruise while Don was getting thirsty. Down at the Rhine they found a cruise boat for dinner cruises that Don thought would do the job. Linda immediately squashed that idea. She was going to have a real Rhine cruise and not just a couple of hours around Mainz on a dinner cruise.

Surprisingly, it took quite awhile to find out where one could get a cruise but eventually they located a large kiosk and made arrangements to be there the next morning for a cruise from Mainz to Koblenz. They walked back to their hotel. By now they were getting tired and Don's feet were beginning to hurt. After what seemed to be an eternity they found their hotel and began to think about supper. A pizza would be good they thought. Don had seen a pizza restaurant just around the corner from the Hotel. Within minutes they were there enjoying a large pepperoni one, which, despite the distance they were from home, tasted very much like the pizza they were used to in Canada. When they left the restaurant they were shocked to see the difference in appearance of the people on the street. Many were young people showing the visible signs of living in the subculture. Don took Linda's hand. "Watch your back," he said as they hurriedly walked back to the hotel. There had been enough excitement for one day and they were tired now. In a very short time they were sound asleep. They were awakened early the next morning to the sound of construction equipment operating. The crew who were rebuilding the Bahnhof were mixing cement and running their cranes. As they looked out the window they could see the city was already awake with people walking everywhere, boarding trains, streetcars or buses. There was already a steady stream of people going into the Bahnhof. They showered hurriedly and packed. After a quick breakfast at the hotel they checked out and were on their way. Don hailed a taxi and instructed him to take them to the KD Cruise Line by showing the driver the brochure. In about five minutes they had arrived and were walking along the dock to the KD Cruise Line kiosk. The man had told Don, the night before, to be there by eight and they were only a couple of minutes ahead of time. A tall Australian was also waiting. When he heard them speak he asked if they were Canadian. When Don said yes he showed them his Canadian passport, then his Australian one. "I live in both countries." he said. It turned out he had been educated at the University Of Toronto and had graduated with an engineering degree in 1950. "I was at your graduation," Don told the surprised Aussie. "What do you mean?" he asked. "My Dad was also an engineering student at U of T and graduated in 1950. I was born a couple of weeks before he graduated and I was at the graduation in my mother's arms," Don said, remembering the story his mother had told him many times as a boy. "Well then, I guess you were!" the Aussie said. "We all graduated together." He told them he was a retired employee of Quantis Airlines and often travelled on his pass. Although he lived in Australia he still had a house in Bowmanville, Ontario (about an hour and a half drive west of where Don and Linda lived) but actually was rarely there anymore. He had only recently lost his wife and this trip was sort of a therapy for him. They spent a fair amount of the cruise talking with each other and Don and Linda enjoyed his company. When the end came at Koblenz he made a point of looking them up to say goodbye. He was, they both thought, truly an interesting and pleasant man. Despite exchanging e-mail addresses they never heard from him again.

As they walked up the gangplank from the ship Don saw a row of taxis parked in a semi circle. Picking the one he thought looked the most helpful he asked questioningly, "Hauptbahnhof, bitte?" (main train station please).

The driver nodded and looked at his watch. Quickly he loaded their bags and they were on their way. Traffic was terrible and the driver fought his way though the crowded streets honking his horn and checking his watch all the way. In about ten minutes they were there. As Don paid the fare the driver pointed to the train sitting in the station. "Schnell! Schnell!" he said. (Quick! Quick!) They hurried up the ramp and onto the waiting train. There were no seats but it did not matter as the train began to quickly move. Standing up was one thing, but the speed of this train was unbelievable. A digital readout in the first class passenger car gave the speed periodically in km per hour. At one point it read 259.9 kps (kilometre pro stunde (stunde=hour). Educated in imperial, Don calculated in his head that they were traveling about 155 mph and standing up at the time. After about twenty minutes they found an almost empty first class compartment. They entered and stowed their luggage in the overhead rack. The lady, who was the only other occupant in the compartment, seemed oblivious to their presence. Linda sat down directly across from her and she hardly stirred. Her face seemed to show some displeasure at their invasion into this private compartment but it was not reserved and they had bought first class rail-passes so Don thought she would just have to live with it. As the train followed along the Rhine retracing the route they had just taken by boat, Linda took pictures of the various castles and towns out the train window. At one point, just as she was about to snap a picture, they passed another train heading in the opposite direction. At these speeds it was a frightening sensation and Linda was visibly startled. The lady had been watching her over the top of the book she was reading but now she began to laugh, slapping her leg in delight. Don had to grin as well as it really was quite funny. From that point on they visited as they rode along. The lady had a reasonable command of the English language and showed them a book she was proofreading for a publisher. Don, who had published his first book (Old Reliable IBSN: 1-55306-35-0)) just a month before, showed her a copy he kept in his suitcase pocket. She seemed dutifully impressed. "Yours?" she asked. Don nodded. She looked through it and looked at both front and back. "My congratulations!" she said handing it back to Don. "Thank-you," he replied and stowed the book away. She asked where they were from and why they were in Germany. They explained Don's family background and also the desire to attend the Oberammergau Passion Play. "Oh, that is very good." she said, "You will enjoy that!" She asked a bit about Don's family and the name. He showed her an old business card he had from his beef cattle business. He had used the old German spelling for the farm. It read Dolmetsch Beef Farm...Don Dulmage. She immediately made the connection. "That is just the English phonetic spelling of the name," she said referring to Dulmage. "So that is why the Pforzheim hotel clerk had known what to look up," Don thought. It seemed to be obvious to the people here. Back home it was almost impossible to explain.

Soon it was time to change trains for the leg from Stuttgart to Munich or, as the Germans say, Munchen. The new train was quite crowded but was also very fast. After two or three stops Linda was able to find a seat. A few minutes later a man who looked very much like Don's friend from home, Lamert DeVries, pointed to Don and then to a spot down the aisle from where he was standing. Sure enough, there was an empty seat against the window. Don leaned over and asked the man if the seat was free. The man who was busy writing in his large notebook pulled his feet back so Don could get in. As they rode along, he worked feverishly in his notebook. Eventually he closed it and put it away. He immediately started speaking to Don in very good English. It turned out he was a business consultant and was going home for the weekend. He was a very interesting person to talk to. They exchanged information on the average wage per person in their two countries and talked for the next hour or so about the different styles of business in Germany and Canada. All too soon it was time for him to disembark. Don found his conversation very enjoyable. As he settled back into his seat he realized they, too, would be at the end of their journey in a few more minutes. Before they knew it the train braked stiffly and rolled to a stop. There were trains and people as far as one could see. Munich or Munchen was the end of the line for the fast trains. Don was stunned at the sheer size of the railway station. It took a bit of time to get their bearings, but eventually they found the side door and headed across the street to a hotel. "This one is expensive," Don thought as he signed in but he was too tired to care. In his mind he calculated they were paying about the equivalent of $300 Canadian if they took it with breakfast or $270 without. Don opted for the cheaper rate. The desk clerk spoke a bit of English but only a very little. Still they managed just fine. Soon they were up in their room resting. After a while they decided to go out and find a restaurant for supper. This proved to be a disaster as they did not know where they were going and the streets were so crowded that they finally had to settle for a hamburger from a Burger King in the front section of the train station. Burger King was well known to them back home and although this was not exactly the same, it was close enough for the moment. The sheer number of people was beginning to wear on Don and he was a bit nervous in this particular part of the station. They hurriedly ate, then returned to their hotel for a good night's sleep. It had been a long and exciting day.

The morning dawned bright and sunny. After a shower they headed downstairs for breakfast. This hotel really knew how to put on breakfast. Besides the traditional German breakfast foods there were Canadian style foods as well. Scrambled eggs and well-cooked slices of Canadian style bacon, little sausages and even toast. Don felt rejuvenated as he cleaned up his plate. Despite the fact that he loved the German food there is something about a Canadian boy (large or small) and bacon and eggs that just naturally belongs together. Somehow he knew it was going to be a great day. After settling their hotel bill they crossed the street to the huge train station. After a bit of checking on the schedule Linda found the train and platform for Oberammergau and they boarded the train and were on their way. They had to change trains at Murnau. Don noticed the trains were getting smaller and a bit rustic. This one, while clean, showed signs of old age and wear. It was also a diesel, which was unusual, as most of the trains they had been on to this point were electric. It moved slowly down the steep track. They looked at each other and shrugged not knowing what to expect. Soon they were rolling along at a reasonable pace. The land outside looked deceptively like Ontario, Canada, where they lived. There were even maple trees in the woods and along the tracks at the various stations. The weeds, the grass and the trees looked very familiar. "If they dropped a Canadian off here and he couldn't see the houses or barns," Don thought, "he would never know he was not in Ontario." It was the first time he had really thought about it and he found it somewhat amazing. Finally the train slowed and came to a stop. "This is it!" Linda said. They grabbed their luggage and stumbled onto the platform. The town was just as they had expected. The guest house nearest the station was closed and was for sale but the rest of the town bustled with activity. They followed the people leaving the train down the main street toward the centre of town. Partway down the street, they saw what looked like a good restaurant. They were not to be disappointed. The food was good and was served promptly. Rejuvenated, they set off again toward the part of town where the play was performed. They spent much of the afternoon shopping in the small shops and then went to the post office to mail some letters. They had decided to visit the town of Wies while they were in the area. Linda's grand-mother had been a Weese and while they were not sure if there was any connection the spelling was close enough and the pronunciation almost the same (except for the German way of pronouncing Ws like Vs) that they decided to visit it just in case a connection was found later on. "Better safe than sorry," Don had said. They called a taxi from the train station. When the lady driver found out where they wanted to go, she called her boss to see if she could get them a reduced fare. Rates were set for traveling around town and it would cost close to 100 DM ($130 Canadian) to go the seventeen km to Wies and back. The answer on the two-way radio was a firm no. Undaunted, Don and Linda swallowed hard and climbed in. It was a once in a lifetime chance and they were not going to miss it. The taxi driver was a Hungarian woman and could speak reasonable English. She was very good to them and took pictures for them as they stood under the Wies village sign. All that was there was a couple of houses and a huge old Catholic church. The driver found it hard to understand that they were only here to see the village and the sign instead of the famous Catholic church. That didn't matter to Don and Linda. Their mission to Wies was now complete and they were ready to return to Oberammergau. Oberammergau has been putting on the Passion Play (life and death of Christ) every ten years since their town was spared from the plague hundreds of years before. All of the actors are from the town and everybody gets into the production of it. People come from all over the world to see it, just as Don and Linda had on this trip. Linda had made arrangements to join a tour group from Kitchener/Waterloo, Canada to see the play. The plan was to meet them in Graswang, which was a small town near the Swiss border. Their arrangements had been made for lodging and for eating as well as transportation to and from the play the following day. They were supposed to be able to get a free city bus to take them to Graswang from Oberammergau but that proved, for a while, to be very frustrating. Finally they found transportation and arrived in a beautiful village nestled right on the edge of the mountains. Their address was 7 Linderhofer str and they found it fairly quickly. While checking in they discovered no English was spoken in that household, but the people were friendly and Don muddled through the checking in procedure just fine. While he was filling out their registration card they heard a lady on the other side of the room exclaim "I don't speak any German, only English!" She sounded a little upset but they could tell from her accent (or rather the total lack of it) that she was Canadian. "Where are you from?" Linda asked her. "Madoc, Ontario, Canada she replied. Don and Linda laughed. Madoc was less than fifty miles from their home in Ameliasburgh. She went on to say she was a teacher. Linda was also a teacher so she quizzed her further. It turned out that her husband was the principal of one of the high schools in Belleville. As soon as Don heard the name he knew who it was. As service manager of a large Canadian Tire garage in Belleville, Don had met many people who worked in town. He knew, from his photographic memory, he had seen that name on at least one work order and had talked to her husband at least once. It was a small world. Luckily for this lady her travelling companion was from Kitchener, Ontario. Kitchener is a bilingual town, but not in the normal Canadian sense (English/French). Kitchener, which used to be called Berlin, was a German-speaking town. This lady was fluent in German and so the problem was quickly solved. Don was very interested in this as his mother was from the Kitchener/Waterloo area and he could remember his grandmother speaking German at the farmer's market and just for fun around the house. She had even taught them to count in German. Soon it was suppertime and they went to the local Gasthaus in the centre of the small village where arrangements had been made for their meals. Because most of these people on their tour were from Kitchener/Waterloo, they almost all spoke German. Automatically they separated themselves out so that those who spoke only English could sit together. One man who came over to sit with Don and Linda was a man named Floyd Neeb. He lived in New Hamburg, Ontario, which was not far from Kitchener. Don knew his mother's family had originally settled in New Hamburg so he told Floyd that. "What was their name?" Floyd asked. "Grandpa was a Daniells, with two Ls and Grandma's people were Stever," Don said. Floyd laughed. "I have a Daniells on one side of my farm and a Stever just down the road on the other," he said. They made plans to

45

meet up in August when the car show was on in New Hamburg but unfortunately it never happened.

After a great meal they walked over to the pasture just across the small bridge. A young farmer was talking to a group of people there as he tried to work. He reminded Don of their neighbour, Brian McFaul, back home with his ruddy complexion and big laugh. Germany or Canada, it didn't matter. Farmers were farmers wherever you go. Good, hard working, friendly folks who enjoy a good laugh now and then. Soon it was bedtime. As they lay in bed, Linda said to Don "I was just thinking, do you suppose this play will be in German tomorrow?" "I don't know," Don said. "I hadn't really thought about it but I guess we are in Germany and so far, right here, hardly anyone speaks English. Why do you ask?" Linda pointed to the playbook she had in her hand. "Well, it is in German with English on the other side. I just thought about it when I saw that. It doesn't matter I guess. The main thing is that I am here and I get to see it. I have wanted to for a long time you know and now we are here." With that they both drifted off to sleep. Morning came early. Don opened the windows in the room as they readied for the day. Soon they were downstairs having breakfast in the guest breakfast room. Other than the people from Ontario that they had met the night before, there was no one else in the room. The food and coffee were all laid out and the table was set in fine style. This was an interesting guesthouse. The living section, including several guest rooms, was at the front of the house in two storeys and the barn, for the cattle, was in the back section. To the uninitiated this may sound a bit frightening, especially by North American standards and yet it was, somehow, just as it should be. The place was scrupulously clean and one could find no just reason to complain. "Besides, it would be fun to talk about back home," Don thought.

With breakfast eaten, they grabbed what they would need for the day and went to the bus stop to wait for their tour bus. When it stopped and Don identified himself and Linda to the tour guide, she seemed unconcerned and welcomed them aboard just like they had always been there. Soon they were in Oberammergau and were receiving their instructions for the day. Things like where to meet for lunch and what would be served as well as when the bus would be returning to their lodgings. They then left the bus and headed for the theatre. After looking around for a while they headed inside and were ushered to their seats. They were almost at the very back of the theatre and fairly high up. Still they could see everything clearly. The only problem was that several people around them seemed to be suffering from colds. They were coughing and blowing their noses. "This is not good," Linda thought, "I know I can't avoid getting a cold surrounded by this." She was right, too, by the end of the day she was sharing in their misfortune. Don somehow escaped. "Germany suited him," he thought. Here he felt sort of "invincible." Of course there was the ever-present problem with his side and he had felt a strange wet sensation in his left foot but he had chosen, for the time being, to ignore it all. Soon the play started. It was a marvellous production probably without equal. Step by step, it went through the life of Christ. It was all in German but the story was very familiar to both Don and Linda and they had no trouble following along. At noon, there was a two-hour intermission, which allowed one to eat lunch and check out the shops along the way. Don and Linda elected to skip the lunch provided by the tour company and instead had rather huge walnut ice cream sundaes at the outdoor cafe just up the street. This would allow them a lot more time to wander through the town and visit the shops before the resumption of the play. It worked out very well and they arrived back at the play just as it was about to resume. The last half was hard for Don. Cramped in a seat designed for a 150 lb person of average height, he soon found his legs were cramping and going to sleep. As the play neared the end he was more than ready for the finish. He gritted his teeth and held on to the last word. As soon as it was done he stood up. Relief flooded over him as the blood again flowed freely in his limbs. Dramas were just not his thing and dramas while cramped in a small seat with no leg room were almost more than he could stand. "Still," he told himself, " this was Linda's big dream so just shut up and endure it." Now it was over.

"What next?" they thought. They spent the rest of the day roaming the town and visiting the shops. It was very interesting. Many shops were selling woodcarvings. Don had been a fairly good whittler with his jack knife when he was a young boy living in Altona, Ontario. However he had not done any whittling in years. Still, this woodcarving held a fascination for him and he did not tire of looking at it. He wondered if he would ever go back to it but didn't really know if he would. "Time will tell, I guess," he thought. As the day wore on they made their way back to the bus and returned to their guesthouse. Soon it was time for supper at the central Gasthaus and restaurant in the village. They joined the same group as the night before. During the meal the conversation drifted to the woodcarving shop up the street. One lady had been there earlier and said the shopkeeper would be staying open later if anybody wanted to go there. That interested Don, so after supper Don and Linda walked to the other side of the small village and into the woodcarver's shop. The quality of the work was incredible. Although the woodcarver spoke no English Don had little trouble making himself understood. Linda had spied a nativity scene carved in a walnut shell (quite literally "the Christmas story in a nutshell") and had decided she wanted to have it. Without much trouble it was purchased and they were on their way back to the guesthouse for a good night's sleep. Time was running out on their trip but they had accomplished so much that they were ready to wind it down. Morning came with the bright sun shining in the window. They ate, said their goodbyes and went to the shuttle-bus stop to get a ride back into Oberammergau. There was a young woman there who was also waiting. The bus never came so eventually the young lady went back to her guesthouse and asked the owner about the shuttle bus. Apparently this route had been overlooked because they thought everyone was on a tour bus but now that they knew there were people waiting the shuttle bus would be there shortly. It didn't take long either before it pulled up and they were on their way back to town.

They boarded the train for the first leg of the journey back to Murnau. After a short wait there they then boarded the next train for Munich. At the huge Munich station they found an apothecary and got Linda some cold medicine and cough drops to help her get some relief from her newly acquired illness. Despite the fact that it was wearing her down, she was able to continue. By now they had the Munich station figured out. They bought the equivalent of some submarine sandwiches and sat on the platform eating them while waiting for the Frankfurt train. At the last minute Linda realized they were in the wrong spot and said to Don "Come on! We should be over there!" She had realized, not a moment too soon, that they had forgotten that German train schedules use the 24-hour clock. Just as they reached the new platform the train rolled in and stopped. Quickly they were aboard and before they had settled themselves in their seats it was underway. They were anxious now and wanting to get home. All, in fact more than they had hoped for, had been accomplished and they were anxious to share their experiences with their friends back home. Once in Frankfurt, they found a room at the Best Western Hotel and then had some supper. They walked back over to the train station to see if they could figure out how to get from Frankfurt Main Train Station to the airport. They knew it was probably obvious to everyone but them, but eventually gave up and returned to the hotel. On the way back Don saw an East Indian man standing outside of an East Indian restaurant. Having several friends of East Indian descent back home Don knew this man would be able to speak English. Sure enough he was right. When asked about the airport the man told them that the simplest way might be just to have the hotel call a taxi to take them. It sounded like a good idea to Don and he thanked the man and they walked on. Soon they were in their room with a wake-up call for early morning arranged. It came very early, too. It seemed like they had just gotten to sleep. They freshened themselves, then dressed and went downstairs for breakfast. It was the typical German style breakfast and while very good Don longed for his Canadian style fried eggs and bacon. Soon they were back in their room with everything packed. Don looked out the window. It was raining hard but, at this point, he didn't care. Home was calling loudly and that was all that was on his mind. The desk clerk called a cab for them then settled up their bill. Soon they were in a Mercedes heading for the airport at the incredible speed of 160 km per hour in the pouring rain. "That is 100 miles per hour," he thought. "These guys are nuts!" They were at the airport before they knew it and were checking in. Everything went smoothly and they were moved on into the holding room waiting to board. They struck up a few conversations with fellow travellers as they waited. Don helped one woman with her bags as they boarded. She had more bags than arms and he had none he was carrying so, against his better judgement, he helped her out. Having lived in many different places, including a three year stint in Montreal, Don had developed a sort of sixth sense about people that had turned out to be fairly reliable and he was satisfied this woman was okay.

Before long they were seated in the plane and taxiing out to the runway. As the plane left the ground Don turned to Linda and said, "Well, that was really interesting but I guess we will never need to come back." His comment shocked Linda. "Never say never!" she said. Little did she know how prophetic that would turn out to be.

Chapter 4

The Search

Don sat down at his computer. He poked around in the search engines entering the old Dolmetsch spelling of his name. Eventually he found himself in with access to the European phone listings. He wasn't sure how he got there but immediately decided to make the most of it. He opened the web page and scrolled to Germany. In the search window he again typed the name. At first it looked like he had thirty-seven results but as he began to investigate he discovered many were businesses that specialized in translation. He knew from his research that that was what the word Dolmetsch meant in German. He printed them all out anyway and then sorted through finding the people named Dolmetsch. He typed up a letter describing who he was and what he knew of his Dolmetsch roots. He invited replies in whatever language they were comfortable with and then printed seventeen copies. He signed every one of them and then stamped them with his web site and e-mail address. This is too easy he thought, but I am going to give it a try. Sitting down he addressed sixteen envelopes and inserted the same letter in each one of them. The next morning he drove down to the local post office to find out how much postage he would need. Soon they were on their way to Germany. Whether for better or for worse he did not know, but he thought it was at least worth a try. Within a couple of weeks he started getting some back. The first one was from Peter Dolmetsch of Munich. He had his daughter write it. Don was not happy reading it. It said that it was absolutely impossible that they were related and Peter had enclosed a chart to prove it. Don looked at the photocopied family tree. All of a sudden his eye caught a number and a name. He had read that some researchers had thought #55A, Joseph Dolmetsch, was most likely his ancestor's (Johann Adam Dolmetsch) father. The trouble was that no one seemed to know who Joseph was or where he fit in. Now, right in front of him, was the same number and name. "55A Joseph Dolmetsch, Sulz geboren 1640." He wondered if it could be the same person. It seemed too good to be true. He ruffled through his stack of files trying to find the paper he had with that information on it. It had come from cousin Reta Selleck but in his excitement he could not seem to find it. It was almost an hour later when he saw it. Sure enough the information matched. It gave four possibilities but said the most likely candidate was #55A Joseph Dolmetsch. As he looked over the sheet he realized he had the family tree right back to 1510. Old Peter may not have wanted to be a cousin, but he sure helped Don out with this chart. Still irritated, Don penned off a reply. It was a bit on the offensive side, but Don thought that it probably would not survive the translation back into German. He made a point of thanking Peter for the missing information. The next day three more letters arrived with "Zuruck!" stamped on the envelopes. Don got out his German dictionary only to discover that meant "Returned." He was saddened inside but not particularly surprised. Life seemed to go that way. "Oh well," he thought, "at least I tried." Still it bothered him for the next few days. About four days later he sat down and turned on his computer. There was another strange e-mail address in the in-box. When he opened it he couldn't believe his eyes. "Linda!" he shouted, "come and look at this!" Linda trudged up the hall from the bedroom where she had been folding the freshly-washed clothes. "What now?" she thought. While she appreciated Don's interest in the computer it seemed he always wanted to show her something at the most inconvenient time. When she got there she was surprised herself. There on the screen was "Hello from Germany." The letter said that the family had received all their letters but unfortunately most did not read English. They had gotten together and were surprised to find that there were Dolmetsch family members in Canada. She went on to describe her immediate family and ended with "Moreover my father would like you and your family to come to our resort in Germany, June 3, 2001." Don had never seen more beautiful words in an e-mail.

"See, I told you!" Linda cried. "Never say never! Now what are you going to do?"

"We're going!" said Don and he turned and smiled. What a day this was. It was almost too good to be true. Over the next couple of days they exchanged information and sent each other family pictures. There were some definite family resemblances between the two sets of photos. After a while things settled down and Don began the long wait until the following June. Right now that seemed a long, long time away.

A few days later Don was checking his e-mail when he saw that characteristic "de" (Deutschland) hanging on the end of another new e-mail address. He clicked on it, curious to see what was inside. It was a request for a copy of his automotive book (Old Reliable) there on his e-mail. "I wonder who that is from?" he thought as he clicked on it. It was from a Mike Schwienbacher (pronounced Shveenbecker) in Germany. That got his attention. Excitedly he printed out the request and the address. He packaged the book and mailed it out the next day. He wrote a note in it saying "In honour of you being my first order from Germany and in honour of the fact that my family came from Germany in 1709, I am donating this book to you." A couple of weeks went by then he saw the same address in his e-mail in-box again. When he clicked on it he saw a note that told him the book had arrived safely and asked did he know that Dulmage was spelled Dolmetsch in German.

The note went on to say there were sixteen in the German phone book.

Don e-mailed back that, yes, he knew and had recently found them himself. He told Mike how he had been invited there the following June and went on to say he had sent a package to them but was unsure if it had actually gotten to the right person. Mike replied that when he had time he would phone. Don was a bit nervous with this for some unexplainable reason, but decided they had nothing to lose. The next morning Mike e-mailed to say that he had talked to Martin Dolmetsch by phone for quite a long time and that they were looking forward to meeting Don. "He is a very nice person," Mike told Don. Mike then went on to say that they did not speak any English. "I will teach you German by e-mail, " he told Don. "Oh yeah," Don thought to himself. "That will really work!" He had never heard of such a thing. Mike, however, was true to his word and began the lessons with the next e-mail. At first it was very frustrating. The dictionary Don was using was not very complete. After hunting around in the local bookstore he came across The Bantam New College German/English Pocket Dictionary, which proved very helpful. And so it was, at the ripe old age of fifty, his education began again.

Chapter 5

Switzerland

ike Dolmetsch had just returned from a hard night's work. As a professional musician he loved his chosen profession but inevitably after a long concert it always took some time to unwind. He slipped out of his jacket and sat down at his computer. Just for fun he typed in his family name to see what would come up. Yes, there was the family business, Messer Dolmetsch. He wondered what life would have been like if he had stayed and taken it over, still, he was glad his father had encouraged him to pursue his passion for music. It was a choice he had not regretted. "Hmm, he thought, "there is a strange one, Don Dulmage." I guess that is close to Dolmetsch. I wonder what that is all about?" He clicked on the title and stretched while his computer loaded. "Dolmetsch, Dolmage, Dulmage, Delmage," it read. "These must be the English versions of our family name," he thought. He read on through the web page. Exactly as he had thought. The person who owned this web page had descended from a Johann Adam Dolmetsch. who left Germany in 1709. "I don't remember that name in Der Stammfogle Der Familie Dolmetsch," he thought, "but it must be the same family. I think I will e-mail him."

He typed a short e-mail and sent it on his way. It seemed strange to see information on his family in Canada. He knew of a couple of family members in the USA, but Canada was not something he had thought about till now. He poked around a bit more, checked his e-mail in-box then shut the computer down and went off to bed.

Halfway around the world only moments later, Don Dulmage turned on his computer and checked his e-mails. "There is a strange one," he thought. "I wonder who that could be?" He clicked on the line and waited for it to load. Much to his surprise it was from a Mike Dolmetsch in Switzerland. This Mike Dolmetsch had seen Don's web page and had e-mailed Don. He gave Don a little bit of the family history in Switzerland and questioned him on the Dolmage/Dulmage spelling. He went on to say that he didn't see that in his copy of the Dolmetsch family tree. Don finished reading the letter and reached in his file drawer for the copy of Der Stammfogle Der Familie Dolmetsch that he had recently received from Martin Dolmetsch in Germany. Using a software program and a German/English dictionary he had translated a large part of it already. He clicked on "Reply" and typed a letter back to his newfound cousin. "While you will find no reference to the Dulmage spelling you will find

mention of Dolmage on page nine near the top of the page."
He gave a short run down of his own family tree remembering especially to put in the section from Gerhardt
Dolmetsch to his son Jacob Dolmage and then to his son
David Dulmage. He was pleased to meet this individual. It
had never occurred to Don that there might be Dolmetsch
people in Switzerland. The next day Mike wrote back that he
had indeed found that reference in the family tree book. "You
seem to know it better than I," he wrote. Don smiled when
he read that. It was probably just the fact that it related to
him directly that brought it to his attention as it certainly
wasn't because he knew the book in any great detail.

Over the next few months they e-mailed back and forth.
Mike sent Don a CD of the music group he was currently
working with. It was Gospel music, which was a favourite
with Don. It was a style of music and songs he was familiar
with so he played it every chance he got. Don discovered
that Mike Dolmetsch was from the same family line as
Martin Dolmetsch in Germany, but Mike's family had gone
to Switzerland and developed their knife store business,
Messer Dolmetsch. (Messer means Knife in German.) Don
was also surprised at Mike's command of the North
American style of English. Mike explained that his girlfriend was from New York and that she had influenced him
in his English speaking. When Mike found out Don planned
to come to Germany the following June he suggested that
Don should also visit Switzerland. The idea of meeting
Mike appealed to Don and he made a mental note to
include it in their plans. Over the next few months Mike
and Don e-mailed each other on a regular basis.

Chapter 6

The Visit

on and Mike Schwienbacher communicated regularly by e-mail. True to his word, Mike began to teach Don the German language. At first, he borrowed lessons from his younger sister's schoolbooks and had Don translate them. Don found this very frustrating but he also knew it was probably his only hope. He had learned some lessons in his life that were especially true for him. He knew he did not learn well in what he perceived as "over-structured" environments such as classroom style instruction. He had taken French for a few years in high school while living in Pointe Claire, Quebec. His father had taken a job there while Don was just beginning high school so he was immediately plunged into having to learn the French language as part of his schooling. Still, he had picked up far more French working in the service station business after school. In fact, although he had not spoken it since 1967, he had been able to communicate with little problem with a man named Eric Goolaerts in France. They had done well enough that Don was able to direct Eric to his Great Uncle Hubert's burial site in a Canadian War Graves Cemetery near Arras, France. He had actually surprised himself with what he remembered. He knew he had a good possibility of learning German with Mike Schwienbacher's home-brew e-mail lessons. He knew it would not be easy. Nothing worthwhile ever was. But he knew if he stuck at it, no matter how distasteful it might seem, eventually he would succeed. Back and forth came the e-mails. Soon they were talking in simple German sentences. Mike found it almost as frustrating as Don but they stayed with it. Then, one day, Mike told Don that he and his father had bought airline tickets for Canada and would be arriving the second week of February. He went on to say they had arranged to stay at a bed and breakfast in a town called Picton. In fact, they were going to stay at "The Blue Spruce." For some reason, Don thought he should know that name. He had lived in Picton for a while in his late teens. It was only about a twenty minutes drive from his home in Ameliasburgh. In fact, many Dulmage family members had lived in Picton over the last 200 years. Don asked Mike where in Picton, "The Blue Spruce" was. Mike directed Don to the web site for the place. When Don saw the web site he could scarcely believe his eyes. "The Blue Spruce" was the name of the bed and breakfast at 26 Lake Street, Picton. It was the very house Don had lived in the whole time he was in Picton. This was a bit hard to believe. When Don told Mike, he was also just as shocked. It seemed almost impossible to have happened just by chance but nevertheless it was true. Don told Mike that he and Linda would pick them up at the airport in Toronto and drive them wherever they wanted to go. He warned Linda later that evening of how busy they would be. "I think, though, dear," he said, "although you may not understand it, I owe this. When my ancestor, Johann Adam Dolmetsch left Germany for England and then Ireland somebody helped him along the way or he would have not succeeded. I am, in just this one small way, repaying the debt." Linda had no problem with that. "Besides, " Don went on, "it will be a great adventure." Linda smiled to her-self as Don spoke. Adventure seemed to be his middle name. Life for this couple had been anything but dull. It had maybe not always gone the way they had planned or hoped but it had never been boring.

Sooner than anyone realized the date arrived and Linda and Don headed up the highway to Toronto to meet their newfound friends in person. Linda had made a large sign from roll-up paper with "Welcome to Canada, Schwienbachers" written on it. Soon they found themselves standing at the arrival gate, holding their unrolled sign, watching for Mike and Sigfried Schwienbacher to arrive. Mike had sent pictures so they knew who they were looking for. After what seemed like forever, the elder Schwienbacher, Sigfried, came walking through the door. When he saw the sign he broke into a huge grin. Don and Linda spotted him immediately as he walked over and joined them. Don tried some of his new German. "Wo ist Mike?" (Where is Mike?) he asked. "Ich weiss nicht."(I know not) said Sigfried pointing to the customs and security door. Don spotted a customs agent who had just come through the door. He asked her about Mike and why he wasn't with his father. Before he got an answer the tall smiling German came strolling through the door. Mike was much taller than they had expected. He also spoke very good English. He was very methodical and did not have any trouble controlling the speed at which he spoke while he searched for the right word. Within minutes they were in the van and underway. Sigfried had brought a video camera and was already busy filming as they left the airport. They got along surprisingly well considering they had just met. A couple of hours later they stopped off at Don and Linda's in Ameliasburgh for some food. Mike took the opportunity to e-mail home to announce their safe arrival. After this short break they made their way to "The Blue Spruce" in Picton. During the next nine days they drove hundreds of kilometres together. Mike and Sigfried were here on a mission. They wanted to buy some property in Canada. It had been a long-time goal of theirs to come here and they didn't intend to waste the time. "First we find some property and then we will do some fun." Mike had told Don. As it turned out, finding and buying the property consumed most of the entire visit, but they had a lot of fun just the same. They looked at many places in Prince Edward County as well as some north of Kingston. Nothing seemed to be working out. Mike had done a lot of online research before coming and so had a folder with all of the places he wanted to see. They had been to Don's lawyer, Ben Van Huizen, to arrange everything should they find an appropriate place. Finally, late in the visit Mike said to Don, "I think there is just one more place to see. It is more than I want to spend but I am running out of choices." He pulled the file from his folder and gave it to

Don. When they arrived at Don's house that morning Don made a couple of phone calls. Soon he had figured out where the place was and they set out to look at it. They missed the turn the first time and so they stopped and asked directions. (This was unusual for Don. Linda wondered what was up. Usually he would drive for hours before asking for directions.) About fifteen minutes later they found the place. It didn't look too bad from the road. There were no buildings on it, but it was certainly in a pretty spot. Mike and Sigi tramped through the knee-deep snow to have a better look. Don and Linda waited in the van to keep warm while occasionally checking to see where their guests were. About a half hour later Mike and Sigi reappeared from the bush. Mike was trying to run in the deep, crusty snow but finally had to slow down and just trudge his way to the road.

"I think we will buy this place," he said. They piled in the van and headed to Belleville. In the real estate office they prepared an offer and then took it to the lawyer to see if it was okay. All was well and they arranged to meet the real estate agent the next day, providing the offer was accepted. There was little chance it would not be as Mike had offered the asking price. He realized time was short and the price was reasonable. To waste time playing the dickering game did not make any sense to him at this point. He wanted this property and he was very quickly running out of time to complete a deal. As it turned out, all went well. The deal was signed and all the paper work delivered to the lawyer's office. In their younger days Don and Linda had bought and sold several houses so Don knew his way around this type of business. Mike was grateful for this as it took a load off of him worrying about how things were done in Canada.

Finding a lawyer to look after it and all the other smaller details would have used up time he just didn't have right now. After opening a bank account in Belleville they returned to the property for one last look before preparing for the next day's return to Germany. It was bitterly cold that day, but somehow, Mike did not seem to care. He had just realized his life long dream. He now owned a piece of Canada. Not just a tiny piece either, but twenty-six acres of woodland with tall trees, rocks, and a reasonable sized pond. Besides, it was far enough away from the city to be a real enjoyable place. It was more than he had ever hoped for. Linda had brought a pair of Canadian flags along for the occasion and they took several photos of Mike and Sigi holding the Canadian flags while standing on their new property. Don watched this all with great interest. It gave him a real insight into how it was for his ancestors when they first came here. Often, in the year to come, he reflected on their expressions on that cold February day.

All too soon the entire nine days had slipped away and they were on their way back to the Toronto Airport for the return flight home. Mike asked Don to stop at the bank in Belleville on the way through town. As they walked in an attempted bank robbery was in progress. Mike was at the far end of the bank picking up some things related to his account, but Don was the next one in line behind the would-be robber. He had sort of overheard the conversation but by the time he realized what was going on the would-be robber had given up his attempt and fled the bank. Nancy, the teller who was approached, handled the attempted robbery well. In spite of her fear she turned and walked slowly from her counter leaving the would-be robber talking to himself. He had no choice now but to leave. As they drove toward Toronto in the van Don explained what had happened to Linda and Mike. Mike explained it in German to Sigi. A few days later Don sent them a copy of the newspaper article about the robbery. There seemed to be no end of excitement this year and it wasn't even two months old yet. Little did he know that for him the best was yet to come. As they parted company at the holding area of the airport Don was shocked at how he felt as Sigi and Mike shook hands and walked through the door to the waiting plane. They had become very good friends in a very short time. He hadn't expected this and it caught him completely off guard. In reality it would not be very long before they would all meet again.

Chapter 7

Reunion

From the Schwienbacher's visit on Don worked hard on his German. It was tough for him but he knew from his life's experiences that if he stuck at it long enough he would achieve some measure of success. Whether it would be enough or not he did not know, but he was determined to be able to communicate in some form. Mike Schwienbacher e-mailed every day but now his mother, Renate Schwienbacher, took a more active role. Don welcomed the extra practice and got up early every day so as to have enough time to complete his German e-mails. Little by little it began to come together. Less and less he had to consult the German/English wordbook to understand. He realized fluency was still a long way away, but he knew he could at least function in the German language. Frank and Hilda Schadlinger, who lived nearby, also pitched in and helped. Frank loaned Don some German language movies. One especially appealed to Don. It was called "Der Letzte Fussganger" and would be a good movie in any language. The subject matter was what one would expect in normal everyday conversation and Don watched it every chance he got. He was surprised that he did not wear out the tape because he had long since lost track of how many times he had seen it. He also had purchased a set of "German on the Go" language tapes and played them when driving his truck or when working in the shop by the house. These he played so often that several of the tapes were so worn they began to develop a slight squeal. Being a ham radio operator (VE3LYX) Don was familiar with short wave radio. He set up a small high quality short wave set in the bedroom by his bed. Every night before he went to sleep he would listen to Deutsche Welle Radio from Germany in the German language. Slowly he began to recognize the words as he heard them. The language was vast and he knew he would not master it in the time before his trip but he knew he would be able to at least communicate. It was good learning new things. He enjoyed the challenge and worked at it unfailingly.

As the time neared for their proposed visit to Germany, Karin Dolmetsch e-mailed to confirm his attendance at the family reunion. Don had a lot of questions for her as he did not want to be in the dark about what to expect. He was surprised and pleased at how direct and complete Karin's answers were. They seemed to think in very similar terms. "Must be that common Dolmetsch blood," he thought with a smile as he read her e-mails. Everything was spelled out in detail. Karin would meet him and Linda at the Metzingen train station between 11:00 and 12:00 noon on June the third. From there she would drive them to her father's resort in Buttenhausen. There they would meet the family. Most of the guests would leave late in the afternoon, but Don and Linda would be staying the night. Her father would make sure they were on the train for Switzerland the next day.

Don had made arrangements with Mike Dolmetsch in Switzerland to meet him the day after. Everything was now falling into place. Michele Solimando was also e-mailing and had arranged to meet Don and Linda in Pforzheim two days later. Everything was now in place for an almost unbelievable meeting of Dolmetsch/Dulmage relatives. It was almost too good to be true and Don braced himself mentally for the disappointment that might come when such unbelievable plans go astray. How it had all come together he really did not know. It was like someone or some force outside himself was drawing them all together. "I wonder," he had once said to Linda, "if old Johann Adam Dolmetsch asked God to reunite us someday. It doesn't seem possible for all this to be falling in place like it is." Secretly, he was surprised that he had been able to make all these contacts. After all it had been some 292 years since Johann Adam Dolmetsch left Germany with his family. As far as anyone knew there had been no contact since. All the books Don had read had led him and others to believe there were no Dolmetsch family people left in Germany. It was the rebel in him that had driven him to investigate anyway. Now things were coming together at a frightening speed. History had not been a strong subject for him in school but this was different somehow. It interested him like little else had in his entire life. "Maybe this is what I was made for," he thought. "Maybe this is my life's mission."

As the time neared for the visit, the Schwienbachers invited Don and Linda to stay with them. After all they were by now good friends and they did live only a short distance from the Frankfurt Airport where Don and Linda would be landing. The idea appealed to both Don and Linda and they quickly agreed. The rest of the trip was now planned. They would go from the visit with Michele Solimando back to the Rhine and would sail as far as practical on the route that Johann Adam Dolmetsch had taken so many years before. When boat travel became difficult or impractical they would switch to the train. The train followed the river anyway so it would be very close to the exact route taken. They decided to go all the way to Rotterdam and then see if they could find a boat from Holland to England arriving as close to London as possible. On the original trip the German refugees had stayed in Blackheath in camps. Don had inquired on the Internet but had discovered there were no remnants or memorials to any of these camps and so if they stayed in the general area that would be the best they could do. From there they planned to go to Ireland, to the area around Rathkeale, where the family had settled. It was a tall order for the short time they had and they realized it might not be possible to fit it all in. In his heart, though, Don had promised himself to give it his very best effort. He had made up his mind that he could stand almost anything if he could pull this trip off.

The time slipped away at an alarming rate and before they knew it they were in an airport van on their way to Toronto for the trip to Germany. Everything went well. The trip over was relatively uneventful. In fact, Don had so much on his mind that they arrived almost before he realized it. Soon they were standing at the baggage claim area waiting for their suitcases to come from the plane. This seemed to take forever. At one point Don looked across the huge room to the automatic door. He could just see Mike and Sigi Schwienbacher standing there, waiting, as the door opened to let someone through. He was not sure they had seen him, but was comforted knowing they were there. Baggage was extremely slow in coming but finally their two small suitcases came around and they gathered them up and headed for customs. Clearing customs went very quickly. So quickly, in fact, that Don was surprised. Soon they were through the door and renewing their acquaintance with Mike and Sigi. It was good to see their friends again, but now the roles were reversed. Mike and Sigi had parked Sigi's Chevy van in nearby Hanau near where he worked. They boarded the train for the short ride to Hanau. From there they rode in the van to Bruchkoebel where the Schwienbachers lived. It was a nice town, very clean and well laid out. When they pulled into the driveway the family came to meet them. Renate, (Mike's mother and Sigi's wife) was quick to make their acquaintance. She had been communicating with them via the Internet but this was their first chance to meet. Mike's sister, Verena, was also there. She was a very quiet girl who stayed in the background but always within earshot. Mike acted as translator. It was a good thing too, as Don was so tired from the trip and so excited to be there that his brain was already, as Mike liked to say, "in standby modus." After greetings and some food Mike said "I think Don is already sleeping. Yes?" It was true. Don and Linda were both so tired they could barely keep their eyes open. It was agreed they would go to their room and take an hour's nap to try to get back on track. The time difference between Toronto and Frankfurt was six hours so the adjustment was quite severe. They lay down in their room and within minutes were sound asleep. When Don awoke he realized that almost two hours had passed by. They freshened up and went downstairs. It was decided they should see the surrounding area before dark and so they all piled in the van and the tour began. First they went to the park, then for a short tour of the Puppen Museum. Next they were off to the Hanau town square where the monument to the famous Grimm brothers was. Don had brought an English copy of Grimm's Fairy Tales for Renate. Interestingly enough she had bought a German copy of the same book for Don. The covers of the two books were almost identical. Despite the language barrier they got along fine. Linda and Renate went to the stores for a while while Don and the rest of the group waited at the Grimm brothers' monument. Don could understand enough German to know what was going on but still many words eluded him. Mike was always quick to translate but occasionally he would ask Don "Do you know what he said?" Sometimes Don did but there were also times he was completely lost. He realized this language learning project was a bit harder than he had counted on. Still some understanding was better than nothing. Later on they toured the grounds of Phillipsruh Palace. Sigi walked behind with Don and spoke to him. With his easygoing manner and the few English words he knew thrown in Sigi was very easy to understand. When Don spoke however he found it difficult to express himself in German. Mike laughed. You just need to be thrown in the German language swimming pool," Mike said, "then you will be okay. It takes some time, so don't worry."

Don envied Mike. He seemed to have an excellent command of English and did not panic as he spoke but picked his words methodically and carefully. He hoped someday he could do as well in German as Mike did in English. Mike's girlfriend, Noiy, was along as well. She had been educated in Thailand and had some training in English. Little by little she began to talk with Linda. The more she spoke the better she got. Obviously she knew the language and one could see with a little bit of practice she would be fine. All too soon the evening came to a close and they turned in for a good night's sleep. Don slept hard. He didn't remember waking up at all in the night. When morning came he opened his eyes slowly. He had still not adjusted to the time change but life would wait for no one so he forced himself out of bed and got ready for breakfast. Linda was not far behind. Mike had agreed to drive them to the area where Don's ancestor, Johann Adam Dolmetsch, had last lived. Don had been able, through several sources, to determine the towns and the areas where his family had lived and worked. It was about an hour and a half's drive south of Bruchkoebel. They piled in Noiy's little red Ford and headed out on the highway. It was raining much of the way and was a bit cool, but no one seemed to notice. Before long they arrived in Alzey. Don and Linda had been here the previous year and so they knew their way around. Don led them to the town square and then to the Evangelische Kirche (Protestant church). He had been here before and told Mike it would be locked. Mike tried the door anyway. "Don, it is open," he said. "Let's go in." Don could scarcely believe their good fortune. From what he knew of the family history he was fairly certain Johann Adam Dolmetsch had also been to and probably inside this very church. The original structure predated Columbus' discovery of America. There were records of Johann Adam having been here in the 1690s and very early 1700s. It was almost unbelievable to be able to go inside. Don signed the guestbook with a short note in German while Mike looked on helping him write in the proper German style. Don wondered if he would hear from the church by mail after he was back home in Canada. Although he did not know it then that was not to be. Next they went up the street to the Katholik Kirche (Catholic church). Don knew that some of the records for his ancestor had been located in that very church. Even though his family were Protestants they had been forced to register their births and family records in the Catholic church. Whatever the religion was of the ruler of the day became the official church for records and such. Unfortunately that church was locked and they could find no one around so they moved on. It was raining again. Don thought back to his previous visit the year before. The weather on that day had been almost identical. They walked about the town for a while. At the local bakery on the corner they bought some buns and pastries as a quick lunch then returned to the car for the trip to Freimersheim.

Freimersheim took a little while to find. A small farming village tucked away in the hills, it was almost completely hidden from view until at last they came upon it. The Protestant church was right at the edge of the village so they made it their first stop. Obviously fairly new along with its graveyard, Don held little hope of finding any family stones here in the cemetery. Still there were lots of names with which he had become familiar from his studies of the family history but as he suspected no one named Dolmetsch was evident there. He was not particularly surprised because he

had surmised from his research that Johann Adam
Dolmetsch did not "belong" in this village so to speak but
had arrived here as a result of some other reason. Don
thought to himself, it must have been love. He himself had
married and stayed in the community or at least very close
to the area his wife Linda had been raised in and so he knew
first hand that was a likely reason for Johann Adam to have
lived here in Freimersheim. There were good records of his
stay here that Don had found in various books. Also the
fact that Johann Adam had left a few short years after his
first wife Anna had died indicated to him, at least, that she
had been the reason for his being here. Don knew much of
this was only speculation and could never, at this later date,
be proven. It was just that it seemed reasonable to apply his
thoughts and life's experiences to his direct ancestor's action
in an attempt to understand them. Besides it was interesting
to think about it. During their whole two hours or so
walking through the old village they saw only a handful of
people, none of whom spoke to them. In fact the only
person who did, was a cleaning service man working on the
Catholic church at the other end of the village who told
Mike it was okay for them to go into that church. Don
doubted Johann Adam had been in that church but it was
still interesting to look inside. Aside from the newer
Protestant church at the entrance to the village it was relatively unchanged since the days when Johann Adam's little
Dolmetsch kids played in the streets. There were some very,
very old buildings there. Still thinking of why his ancestor
had left this place Don asked Mike what he thought. "It is
hard to say," Mike offered. "There could be many reasons.
Maybe there was just not good enough opportunities here."
Don valued Mike's thoughts as he knew the tall German

was facing similar thoughts himself as he contemplated his own future. He was glad Mike had agreed to bring them here. He had a perspective on things that Don would not have enjoyed had he and Linda come here alone. They walked almost every street in the small village finally finishing up by the farm store. Don was surprised at how much it looked like the Co-op store in Foxboro, Ontario where he had dealt while in the cattle business. He was comfortable in these surroundings and it was a very special experience to be here walking around the actual village where your ancestor had lived. He took a lot of pictures and shot a lot of footage on their video camera. He wanted to remember this place. Secretly he wished he had been able to talk with some of the town's residents but that was not to be and so he dismissed this minor frustration and drank in all the sights and sounds of the visit. After a refreshing snack and an orange drink from the cooler Noiy had packed in the trunk of the car, they were again underway. Don had learned that Johann Adam's first wife had died and the funeral had been held in Framersheim some twelve to fifteen km away. Many researchers had thought that Framersheim and Friemersheim were the same place and only a misspelling but Don had learned from his visit to Alzey the previous year that they were two separate towns. Framersheim seemed a lot bigger to Don. They walked around this town for an hour or so. Don had no trouble finding the Protestant church where researchers said Anna Dolmetsch's death records were kept and the original funeral was held. There were no Dolmetsch names in the graveyard to be found. The church was locked and the streets were empty. After a good tour of the area they started back toward the car. As they walked up the street a black car backed out of a courtyard in front of them. Don looked up on the wall as they waited and saw the name Schweizer. He recognized it immediately as the Dolmetsch family and the Schweizers were related by marriage. Their respective names had been changed in spelling to Dulmage and Switzer when they lived in Rathkeale, Ireland. In fact, Don knew some Switzers and their descendants in the area where he lived near Belleville, Ontario. Mrs. Schweizer was closing the gate after her husband had left with the car. When she saw Don's camera she disappeared from sight. He clicked it anyway but, as he later found out, it was too late. Her presence had escaped being recorded. Don would have liked to have talked with her but after seeing her scowl he thought better of it. "I leave that job for those with the actual Schweizer or Switzer name," he said to himself. After a long drive they arrived at an American military base near where Mike and Noiy lived. Although they couldn't go on the base proper Mike informed them that there was a Kentucky Fried Chicken store across the road from it and they were going there. "You can order in English," he told Don. "She will understand okay." Don had some Deutsche small change that Hilda Schadlinger had given him for, as she put it, "lemonade" (pronounced lemonada). He put it to good use and ordered one with their meal. While not exactly the same as the Kentucky Fried Chicken at home it was close enough considering they were in Germany. It was a full-fledged Kentucky Fried Chicken place though, with the pictures of "The Colonel" and all the other things one would expect to find at a "KFC" back home. After the meal they went to the train station to check the schedule for the trip to Metzingen the next morning. A young lady greeted them when they walked in. "Kann Ich halfen?" (can I help), she asked. "Sprechen Sie Englisch?" (speak you English), Don asked. "Bischen" (a bit). she answered. Don swallowed hard and went for it in German. "Wie komm Ich noch Metzingen?" (how come I to Metzingen). "Wenn?" (when) she asked. "Heute oder?"(today or). "Morgen" (tomorrow), Don said. "Morgen frueh (early tomorrow)," Mike interjected realizing what Don was thinking "morning" or "tomorrow," both of which could be said by the same German word needed clarification. Without hesitating the young lady printed out a route advisory and reviewed it with Don and Mike. Don realized for the first time that despite his limited ability with the language he would be able to function okay. He would just have to take it real slow and keep it simple. As they drove to Mike's home, Mike said, "I think we will drive you tomorrow, Don." "That is not necessary," Don said. "It is not about necessary," Mike said. "We will see what happens in the morning." Don didn't argue. He was tired but satisfied with their success this day. After a good night's sleep maybe it would be easier to decide. That night Mike, Noiy, Sigi and Renate as well as Mike's maternal grandparents, Hugo and Lilo, treated Don and Linda to a feast on their terrace the likes of which Don and Linda had never seen. It was so good that Don ate so much he thought he would burst. This bothered him a bit as so far he had not seen any German people yet who were as big as he was. To add this extra to it worried him but it was some of the best food he had tasted and so he released himself from his self-imposed restrictions and sampled everything at least once. Soon it was bedtime and morning would come early. Don needed something from downstairs after everyone had gone to bed. Sigi was still in the kitchen when he went down. Don asked for what he needed in German and explained why. Sigi just smiled and nodded and returned with the requested item. Don was pleased that he had been able to communicate the meaning he had intended. Soon they were fast asleep. It had been a long but exciting day.

Chapter 8

Face to Face

on awoke slowly the next morning. Linda was already stirring. Slowly they took turns getting ready for the day. Don was a bit apprehensive to say the least. He could hardly believe that today he would actually get to meet the descendants of his original Dolmetsch family who had stayed behind in Germany. He knew that many of his friends who knew they were coming here did not seem to realize the significance of this event. The two (Canadian and German) family groups had not had any contact with each other since 1709. Up until last year it seemed neither even knew that the other existed. He himself had been led to believe that there were no Dolmetsch people left in Germany and yet here he was just hours away from reuniting with the family. A thousand "what ifs" went through his mind. "What if they didn't care?" he thought, but in his heart he knew if that was true they wouldn't have invited him to come. "What if they think I am not from their family?" he thought. That had the same answer as the first question. He had also seen photos of them and there was an unmistakable family resemblance. "What would they be like in person?" Maybe he had just talked himself into thinking they looked like family. He dismissed that thought as the pictures spoke for themselves. Finally, he made his way downstairs for breakfast with Linda following close behind. The rest of the household was already up and breakfast was on the table. As they ate Mike explained that he had talked it over with Sigi and they had found everything on the map. He showed Don the marked copy. "We will drive you today," he said.

"But it's so far." Don said.

"It is nothing," Mike said in his matter of fact way. Don knew it was useless to argue and was secretly glad Mike would be along when he met his original Dolmetsch family. Time seemed to fly and in a flurry of activity, good-byes were said and they were driving up the street in Noiy's red Ford. Noiy was in the back with Linda and Don sat up front with Mike. As they drove the weather went from rain to sunshine and back again. After quite a while Mike pointed to a road sign announcing they had just entered the Wurttemberg area of Germany. "We are in Dolmetsch-land now," he said as he looked at Don and grinned. He could tell Don was having a hard time with this and was determined to help his friend realize his dream. "This is very important to Don," he thought. Don was very quiet and Mike knew he was stressed out.

As they rode along Don thought back to a book he had read when in his early teens. It was called "Dr Livingstone, I Presume" and was about Henry Stanley's search and discovery of the famous missionary, Dr. David Livingstone. To Don, this upcoming meeting would be very similar. How he hoped nothing would go wrong. When they stopped for gas near Stuttgart, Mike checked the map. Mike and his father, Sigi, had gone over it thoroughly and all the turns and Autobahn numbers were clearly marked. His father knew about such things, that was for sure. Soon they were in Stuttgart and driving by the Porsche factory. Maybe on some other day they would have stopped and looked around, but not today.

As they pulled up to the traffic light the road signs were not clear. Mike took a minute to look at the map and the signs. He looked at his watch and then at Don. "Soon," he said with a grin. "I am not exactly sure which direction to go. If it is not this way then we will know soon enough." They drove for a few more minutes through Stuttgart. All of a sudden Mike saw a sign that indicated they had made the wrong choice. No one was coming so he immediately made a U-turn and headed back the way they had come. He checked his watch. Time was running low. They were to meet Karin Dolmetsch at the Metzingen train station between 11 and 12 hours. It was already just past 11 and they were still in Stuttgart. They had enough time, he knew, but no time for mistakes. He remembered Don telling him that Karin had told him to phone when they got close. He pulled into a parking place near the corner and pulled his cell phone from his pocket. "I think we must phone now," he said. Don gave him the number. He dialed it carefully and handed the phone to Don. Don could hardly hear as his heart was pounding in his chest. Almost immediately after the ring he heard a voice saying "Karin Dulmage." Actually he knew she had said Karin Dolmetsch but the pronunciation was exactly the same as the way he said his own name in Canada despite the difference in spelling. He spoke to Karin but she said. "I am sorry, I can not understand you." He panicked a little. "What would he do now? She didn't understand him." Mike grabbed the phone and stepped out of the car. As he talked the tall man walked up and down the sidewalk. He knew immediately, from the look on Don's face, what was wrong. The phone was just not doing a good job from inside the car around all these buildings. He arranged with Karin that he would drive to a store or public place in Metzingen and then he would call her again. She knew the whole town well as she had lived there her entire life. She would know where Mike was when he called. Mike stepped back into the car. "She said she couldn't understand me," Don said. Mike nodded. He understood Don's words. "She means she couldn't hear you," he said.

"Because I was in the car with the phone?" Don asked. Mike nodded. He knew exactly where to go now and wasted no time in getting there. About a half hour later he pulled the little red Ford into the parking lot of a shoe outlet. Metzingen had lots of factory outlet stores and this looked like a place Karin would know. As he parked he pulled his phone from his pocket and called Karin. He was right. She knew exactly where they were and would be there in just a few minutes. It was raining steadily now and was a bit cool. He looked over at Don. Don did not look cool at all. Mike could see the strain in his eyes.

"This part is very hard for you, Don," he stated.

"Yes," said Don as he peered through the rain. In a few

minutes an older green Mercedes hardtop pulled up followed by a black VW. Don saw that Karin was driving the VW. He recognized her from the pictures she had sent him. He got out of the car but Karin stayed in hers for a few seconds. The door of the Mercedes swung open and a tall young man in his thirties stepped out. Don recognised him immediately as Karin's brother, Marc Dolmetsch. He walked over and shook Marc's hand. Mike snapped a picture on Linda's camera right at that moment. It seemed the right thing to do for such a historic meeting.

Marc Dolmetsch and Don Dulmage shake hands as they meet in Metzingen for the first meeting of the two lines of the family in 292 years.

"Marc Dolmetsch, I presume," Don said. Now he knew how Henry Stanley felt. It was almost unbelievable to see these living, breathing members of his family. This was the first known contact of the two family lines in almost three centuries. As he turned to Karin she grinned. "Karin," Don said "Give me a hug!" She walked over to Don as he put his arm around her. He was bigger than she would have thought but otherwise he seemed just like she had envisioned he would be. It was raining hard now. Mike began to unload Don and Linda's luggage from the car. Linda and Noiy were talking to Karin and the tall young woman who was with her. She was Marc's girlfriend, Mayella, and seemed to be a very friendly person. Don noticed that she spoke excellent English.

Watching Mike unload the luggage and looking at the rain, Marc said to Mike, "why don't you two come along as well. It is not far and we will unload the luggage later when we get there." Mike hesitated. He wasn't quite sure what to say. Marc pressed the point. "Come on. You will be more than welcome." With the rain coming down and all, Mike finally agreed. "I will take Don and Linda with me," Marc said "and you can follow me or Karin." Mike nodded. As they got into the Mercedes and pulled away Don noticed for the first time that Marc spoke absolutely perfect English. Not a trace of an accent even to Don's Canadian ears. Don asked Marc about it.

"I worked in England for a few years after university," he said. It was a reasonable explanation but it still surprised Don that Marc did not speak with at least a British accent if he had learned to speak it there. It fascinated Don as he thought how Marc had already done some of the things Don's ancestor Johann Adam Dolmetsch had done. Moved to England and learned English. As they talked they compared notes on the family. Don discovered that many of the German relatives had degrees after their name. In Canada, Don explained, they had both tradesmen and engineers and such in the family. As a mechanic, Don was proud of his choice of profession and was always ready to defend the tradesmen's honour if need be. He wondered if Marc thought they were a bit backward but decided not to think about it. He could well remember the attitude many Brits had had towards Canadians as they came in droves to "The Colonies" in the 1950s. He hoped Marc and other Europeans did not have similar opinions but decided not to waste an otherwise perfect day thinking about it. Before long they started up a long sloping hill. As they turned the corner part way up Marc began to brake and soon the car rolled to a stop.

"This is it." Marc announced.

By now it had stopped raining. Mike and Noiy pulled up followed closely by Karin and Mayella. They unloaded the luggage and walked down the steps to the house set high on the hillside. As they entered they could hear the sound of many conversations.

"Yep, they are Dulmages for sure," Don thought. Back home in Canada he had often heard Linda comment about this after they had been to see his family. "Everybody is talking," she had said "and some are even involved in more than one conversation." Don felt immediately at home. Karin showed them to their room and showed them where the bathroom was. Don and Linda stowed their luggage in the room and did what was necessary, then made their way upstairs. Mike and Noiy were already there talking with the family. Martin made his way toward Don.

"Herr Dolmetsch von Kanada, ja?" he said.

"Ja," said Don as he reached out and shook Martin's hand. He liked his distant cousin immediately. With Karin's help, Martin showed them around. Soon Mike Schwienbacher approached Don and said "I think we will go now. Everything is okay and we have a long way to go. Do you know you can tell they are your relatives?" he told Don.

"Really?" Don asked. Mike nodded and smiled. He was glad this was working out for his Canadian friend. Don found Linda and they met Mike and Noiy in the foyer. It was hard to say goodbye to such good friends. Noiy stood teary-eyed as they shook hands and hugged. They had made a lot of good memories together in a very short time. All too soon they were gone and Don and Linda returned to the reunion upstairs.

Before long Martin had Don seated at the end of the living room coffee table. On the table was a picture of Don's family from his parents' fortieth wedding anniversary, which Don had sent to Martin shortly after Karin's first e-mail. Ulrich Dolmetsch was seated by Don with Albrecht next to him and Martin at the end. Albrecht asked Don about each family member in the anniversary photograph. Don found Albrecht fairly easy to talk with even though he asked Don questions in German. Ulrich, who sat closest to Don had a good command of English and stepped in to clear up any misunderstandings. Don found Albrecht to be a very likeable and enthusiastic person. One by one Don identified each member of his family when asked. Later as the conversation drifted to other things Albrecht began leafing through the large photo album of his German relatives and ancestors. The book had been brought to the gathering by Albrecht's first cousin, Wolfgang Losch. Don believed it had been Wolgang's mother's album. She would have been Martin and Albrecht's father's sister (their aunt) and would have been a Dolmetsch before marriage. All of a sudden Albrecht jumped up and tugged on Don's shirt-sleeve. "Don, Don, da bist Du!" (Don there are you). Don looked and could scarcely believe his eyes. There in their photo album of their German ancestors was a picture of a Dolmetsch man who was the absolute spitting image of Don. His hair had waves in exactly the same place and it was the same wild, uncontrollable type of hair. Also his eyebrows were only half eyebrows, something Don also had that had bothered him a bit when looking at himself in the mirror. The man in the photograph had a minor injury or scar on his chin but otherwise he looked exactly like Don. Don was stunned. Not knowing what to say he pointed to his hair and said. "Nicht so grau" (not so grey).

Martin jumped up and headed for his study. He held up his hand and said, "eine moment, eine moment!" (one moment, one moment). Seconds later he returned with a photo Don had sent him of Don before his hair began turning grey. The Dolmetsch men passed around the photo Martin had just brought. The resemblance was amazing. Albrecht looked at Don and then at Martin.

"Genau!"(exact), he said. Martin nodded.

"Ja, genau."

Don asked Martin who the man in the old picture was. Martin explained to Don that it was a Dolmetsch ancestor whose name he did not know but it was definitely a Dolmetsch man as that was all that was in this book. Probably one of their great uncles. After checking with his cousins Martin told Don that the photo was between 100 and 130 years old. There was no denying that Don and the Dolmetsch ancestor in the photo shared some common genes and from that point on any doubts anyone had on the subject of Don's relationship to this particular family in Germany were laid to rest. Don had to admit himself that he had never seen a picture anywhere in his entire life of anyone who looked so much like him. Martin and Don decided to try and get a picture from the picture. Martin took the photo album out onto the terrace and crouched down with it open toward the sun while Don took several photos of it over his shoulder.

Later in the afternoon Don went to his suitcase and brought out some family histories from his side of the ocean. He had written a short piece on the family history from Freimersheim, Germany to Ireland and then to North America and Canada. He had used a computer program (Babelfish) to do a rough translation of it to German and had then sat down with his German/English wordbook and smoothed out the obvious wrinkles. Everybody wanted a copy and soon Don had only one left. Ulrich was reading his copy a little later on. Don told him about trying to translate the history into German.

"Is it readable?" he asked Ulrich.

"Actually it is okay," said Ulrich. "It is very understandable."

Don was surprised. When he had translated it he was just beginning to learn the German language and so he thought it might just be a mixed up mess. The Dolmetsches seemed to enjoy it. Don was glad he had made extra copies. Later on one of the family brought Don into the kitchen. Wolfgang Losch was there and had a very old family tree chart spread out on the table. Claudia Dolmetsch was helping him hold it as he explained the different relationships. Carefully he asked Don in German where he thought his Canadian family fit into the family chart. Don told him he believed that his direct ancestor who had left Germany, Johann Adam Dolmetsch was the son of Joseph Dolmetsch of Sulz. He explained he could not be absolutely certain but that it was most likely the case. He explained that others before him had thought the same thing. In fact, he had included that research in his little family history he had just given them. Not easily persuaded Wolfgang pressed further. Don indicated to him that Joseph was the only Dolmetsch man who had not registered his children by name, but only by their date of birth. He had found from his research no other Dolmetsch man with incomplete records. Wolfgang checked the chart and then nodded. Still, it was going to take more persuading than this. Don went on to say that he could find no other male child recorded as born in the year 1678 except for Joseph's child number five. That was also Johann Adam Dolmetsch's recorded birth date. In actual fact there had been none born even the year before or the year after. Wolfgang seemed to understand. He checked the chart and there, just as Don had said, was a birth recorded as 1678 but with no name given under Joseph Dolmetsch's family records. He checked the other entries on the chart and then acknowledged that seemed to be the truth. After a few more minutes he asked Don where he thought it should be entered and Don pointed to the spot with the unnamed child. Wolfgang checked everything again and then picked up his pencil and began to enter the information from Don's family tree. Strangely enough there was a big empty triangle below Joseph's name but as he hand-entered the data the chart took on a more normal appearance. Don explained that he could not be absolutely sure but that was most likely the case. Wolfgang nodded. He seemed to Don to be satisfied with the explanation and would enter it in pencil for now until it could be better verified. Don mentioned the photo Albrecht had found in the old book. Wolfgang smiled and nodded but still Don knew he was being very cautious.

It did not bother Don as he understood how important it was to be as accurate as possible with the old family records. Still the photo from the old book had to carry some weight. It was plain to see they were definitely from the same bloodline.

All the time this was taking place Linda had been busy taking photographs and shooting video. She wanted to have a good record of this day when they arrived back home in Canada.

Later as Don and Linda were sitting eating at the coffee table in the living room, Paul-Ludwig Dolmetsch, the other brother of Martin and Albrecht, came in and sat down. He explained in English, as best he could, that he had been to Canada in the 1970s and proceeded to name all of the capitals of each province in the proper sequence from east to west. Don was impressed. He liked this man as well. He was quiet and friendly. Don noticed that he was somewhat taller than his brothers. Don wished in his heart that some of them would come to Canada to visit now that they knew they had family there. He expressed this feeling to them and they allowed that it was a possibility. The Dolmetsches were very gracious hosts. Never once did they leave Don and Linda sitting alone but took turns visiting with them. Always there was someone there as well who could speak a bit of English. Linda and Gisela (Martin's wife) were both retired schoolteachers and they discussed as best they could the merits of retirement.

"How many years teaching?" Gisela asked Linda at one point.

"Thirty-five years," said Linda.

"Thirty-five years," said Gisela. "That is enough!" Linda nodded.

Don was impressed that these people tried so hard to speak English with them. He learned that most of them had taken some English in school but very little. He surmised that Gisela, being a teacher, probably had a bit more and had maybe even taught it to her classes. Whatever the case was she made an effort to speak it and did a pretty good job of it as well. During the meal Marc and Don got into a discussion on Canadian food. Marc was basing his point on his experiences during a trip to California and Don set out to remind him that California was no way to judge Canada. Don could see from the gleam in Marc's eye he was enjoying the discussion immensely.

"You are just like my brother Ron," he told Marc. "You enjoy a good discussion." Don noticed as well, that Marc was a worthy opponent in any discussion and could think fast on his feet. For Don it was a lot of fun and he was sure Marc had enjoyed it as well. Because of Marc's perfect command of the English language he had no trouble holding his own.

"Must be in the bloodlines, this discussion thing." Don thought to himself.

All too soon the day came to a close. One by one the people came to shake hands and say goodbye. One man, in a blue shirt, stood out in Don's mind. Although he did not speak any English he had managed to put together enough words to shake Don's hand and say "Donald Karl Dulmage, it was a pleasure to meet you." Don tried to answer back in German but he was now too tired or as his friend, Mike Schwienbacher would often say, he was in "standby modus."

Don and Linda were ready for bed. The jet lag was behind them but now they needed to catch up on their sleep. Still, for Don it was hard to drift off. Here he was, in the land of his forefather, in the summer home of his forefathers and he had just spent the day meeting many of the remaining German members from which his Canadian family had come. What time he finally drifted asleep, he did not know. He guessed it was somewhere around 1:30 am. He awoke to sound of singing birds. It was also like this at home. Once he heard the birds singing that was the end of sleeping for him. Soon Linda stirred beside him.

"What time is it?" she whispered.

"I don't know," he said "but I'm getting up." Slowly they got dressed and headed for the washroom to get ready for the new day. They could hear nothing around them but they were on a floor by themselves so that didn't surprise them. Finally they were ready and headed upstairs. "Whoops!" thought Don. "No one else is up yet." They walked to the living room and sat down together on the couch. After a few minutes they heard someone coming down the stairs. It was Gisela. She was startled when she saw them and motioned to them then went back upstairs. Soon she returned dressed for the day. She immediately headed for the kitchen.

"Kein schlafen?" (no sleeping), she asked.

"Nein," (no), Don replied. "Wir immer aufstehen mit die vogelen" (we always get up with the birds). Gesla grinned.

"You are a good liar," she said in English and they all laughed. It was however, for Don, actually true. He rarely, if ever, slept on once the morning birds started singing. Gisela gave them some newspaper clippings and a church bulletin to read while she set about making breakfast.

"Can I help?" Linda asked.

"No," came the immediate reply." You are our guests."

Linda thought to herself how direct these people were when asked a question.

"That must be where Don gets this from," she thought. "It really is part of his heritage."

Don, while not a mean person, had rarely left anyone in doubt about what he thought in any given situation. Sometimes he was so forthcoming that it shocked her but now for the first time she began to understand it better.

"It is just part of the gene pool," she thought." Part of his German heritage."

She watched Gisela as she readied breakfast in the next room. This woman had done all the cooking and all the preparation for thirty-five guests the day before. Linda had watched her several times as she had loaded the dishwasher between moments of cooking the sausage, the fish and later the special white sausage. Gisela certainly knew how to be a hostess. "Martha Stewart" (a famous American hostess in the 1990s), thought Linda, "Eat your heart out!" When it came to being a great hostess Gisela Dolmetsch took a back seat to no one! Linda was glad that she liked Don's newfound relatives. She had wondered what they would be like but all that was behind her now. These were truly very nice people.

Soon Karin and her man, Eberhard, showed up. Karin looked a little tired but said hello with a smile.

Martin came down and immediately sat down beside Don with a very old and large book. He spoke slowly with Don in German. Without realizing it Don understood every word. The book was the journal from the leather business in Sulz. Martin explained it had been run by an uncle but none of his children had stayed so the business had passed to Martin's family line. Don was astounded. So much so that he never did say much. He knew from information Michele Solimando had given him that Joseph Dolmetsch (most likely Johann Adam's father) had run a leather business in Sulz. He also knew that Johann Adam had not stayed, but had strayed north before leaving Germany. There was little evidence that any other sons of Joseph Dolmetsch had survived, although his daughter, the eldest child, certainly had as he had seen records of her marriage. Another piece of the puzzle fell into place. As he leafed through the book he could see the actual handwriting of his ancestor Joseph Dolmetsch. Actually, there were several Dolmetsch entries in the book as well as many other names from whom hides had been purchased or leather sold. Don checked the dates, which were meticulously recorded with each entry. The book went from about 1723 to the 1800s. Several different people had made entries as was evident from the different handwriting. Don realized the journal was from a time long after his ancestor Johann Adam Dolmetsch had gone to Ireland in 1709 but it was, never-theless, a significant piece of family history. Next, Martin showed Don a church bulletin from the cathedral in Ulm. He thought Don should go with him sometime and they could climb the tower, all 700 and some steps.

"That's too many for me" Don said in German and they both laughed. Don secretly hoped he and Martin could someday go there together and at least visit it. He knew all three of the Dolmetsch brothers, Paul- Ludwig, Albrecht and Martin were architects. In fact the house they were in, high on the hillside, provided ample evidence of Martin's architectural abilities. It had an inordinate amount of wood in it and was a very unusual design but was still somehow very "homey." Don really liked his newfound German rela-tives. They were without a doubt genuinely nice people.

"Okay!" Gesla called.

Martin motioned Don and Linda to the kitchen table. He motioned to Don to sit in the chair at the end. Don refused.

"Konigs stuhl" (kings chair), he told Martin. He had been raised to respect the place the head of the household sat in at the table. In his own home, as a boy, and in the Mennonite homes of his neighbours no one ever sat in the father's chair. Even in his own house he always, without fail, maintained his spot at the end of the table. Not even his father, when visiting, could sit there. He was not about to change that now. Martin seemed to understand and smiled. Don slid in beside Linda, but next to Martin. As they ate, Martin reached for a wooden tea box. Don noticed it right away as they had some similar ones at home in Canada. Martin removed a small pill from the box.

"Fuer blutdruck" (for blood pressure). He looked around for someone to translate.

"Ich verstehe" (I understand), Don said. "All Dolmetsch man sind so" (all Dulmage men are so). "Nicht sehr gut" (not very good) said Martin.

"Es ist gut fuer die Artzt" (it is good for the doctor), said Don.

Gisela laughed out loud. "Gut fuer die Artzt," she repeated and shook her head. It was good for everyone to share a laugh together. Don and Linda then talked a bit with Karin. One of the things that were common to many Dulmage people in Canada were their eyes. When Don was younger and living in Picton, Ontario, older people would often ask him if he was a Dulmage. When he would ask how they knew they would invariably say you have the "Dulmage squint." Karin had those same eyes that many of Don's relatives in Canada had. It was interesting to see how some of these bloodline traits were the same on both sides of the ocean.

Martin Dolmetsch and his daughter Karin Dolmetsch pose with their Canadian cousin Don Dulmage to show how they all have the same Dolmetsch/Dulmage eyes.

All too soon breakfast came to an end and Martin stood up. Everyone else did as well. Matin and Karin explained to Don and Linda that Eberhard, Karin's man, would be driving them to the Stuttgart train station rather than have them take the train from Metzingen. That would save them a stop on their way to Zurich, Switzerland. Don did not argue. He now trusted these folks completely.

In what, for some reason seemed like a blur, they found themselves outside loading their suitcases into the back of Eberhard's BMW. Don gave Karin a hug and thanked her for putting it all together. He was convinced that without her this visit would probably not have taken place. He shook hands with the rest and said goodbye. It had been a great visit and had exceeded even his wildest dreams. He hoped they had enjoyed it too and wondered if he would ever see them again. Karin was driving the older Mercedes back to Munich so Eberhard could work away on it for a while and get it back in tiptop shape. They had brought it out just for this special occasion as they knew Don was interested in cars but had now decided to bring it back to its original condition. Don was impressed that they had gone to such lengths for his visit. He was pleased to be related, no matter how distant, to such fine people. Soon the house disappeared from view and they began the journey to Stuttgart. It had been a short visit but a full one, with no regrets. Don felt somehow complete within. It was hard to put into words, but it was "okay."

As they drove Eberhard began to talk to Don about cars and engines.

"I wrote a book about that," Don said after a while, "and I sent copy to the family over here." "Yes I know," said Eberhard, "I have it at my office. I wish it was in German as it is hard for me to read these things in English."

"What is your profession?" Don asked.

"I am an engine design engineer for BMW racing." Eberhard said.

Suddenly Don's little book on his homebrew racing car seemed insignificant.

As they drove they talked quite a bit. Don could see why Karin liked Eberhard. He seemed like a decent and very intelligent young man. As they pulled into the parking lot at the train station Eberhard offered Don a bottle of non-alcoholic wine as he knew Don and Linda were non-drinkers. As hard as it was to do Don graciously passed it up. Later he wished he had done differently but the thought of carrying a glass bottle with them on their journey seemed at the moment too difficult to deal with. In his heart Don hoped desperately that he would understand and not be offended. Eberhard showed them to the proper platform then shook hands and vanished from view. Don knew he was someone he would not soon forget.

Now, as they waited for the train to Zurich they took in the sights and sounds of the train station. It was a national holiday and people were travelling everywhere. Don watched as people looked at them. He knew they could tell that he and Linda were foreigners. If asked he would have found it hard to explain but he knew full well that back home he could pick non-Canadians out with ease. He was sure that it was no different for the German people here. Subconsciously he flipped his Canadian baggage tag out so it would be in full view.

"We wouldn't want to be mistaken for that other variety," he thought to himself, but just then the train pulled up. They took a few moments to survey the situation and then picked a car and climbed aboard.

Despite all the people in the train station the train was relatively empty. They stowed their luggage at the back and sat down near the rear of the car. Almost immediately the train was underway. At first they slept for a bit and then they talked. As they were talking Don saw the name Sulz flash by the window. They checked their train schedule but could not find it on the list of stops. Still Don was satisfied. He had not yet investigated how they would go to Sulz but at least now he knew where it was. The town north of Sulz was Horb and it was evident that the train stopped there. In fact it just had stopped there a few short minutes before.

"That would be close enough," Don thought. "We can find our way there by bus or taxi if need be."

For the moment, their destination was Zurich, Switzerland, for a meeting with Mike Dolmetsch, Don's Swiss relative. Karin had talked with Mike by phone the day before, just to make sure all would go well. She told Don that Mike's father, Ulrich, had been to one of their family reunions but that Mike himself had never been there. They hoped he would come next year as she had invited him. Before long they crossed the border into Switzerland. Immigration officials walked through the train checking the passports and IDs of the passengers. Don and Linda got theirs ready but when the inspectors reached them the one inspector motioned to them to put them away.

"Kanadier?" (Canadian) he asked, "oder Amerikaner?"

"Kanadier," Don said.

With that the inspector just smiled and stepped through the door into the next car.

"It must be printed on our foreheads," Don thought." How did he know that?"

Soon they made their first stop in Switzerland. Here the train crew changed for the day. The stop took quite awhile and Don could feel himself getting nervous. After what seemed an eternity they were again under way. Tickets were checked as they travelled. Nobody seemed to be too stressed. Don and Linda both liked travelling on these German trains. They were always clean and were very well run. This particular train took them deep inside Switzerland from Germany and all on their German rail-pass. It seemed almost too good to be true but it was.

"No wonder these countries do so well economically," Don thought. "Their transportation system has to be the best in the entire world. If we could move people and goods this efficiently in Canada it would be a totally different place."

At home the government had closed many of its rail lines. He wondered if they had really thought that policy through. They might have saved some money directly from not running the trains to the small towns off the main lines but he wondered if the lost revenues from lost jobs and the income tax they produced was costing far more than anyone realized. He was still thinking about it when the train came to the end of the line.

The Zurich train station was huge. It was also clean and bright. Don looked for Mike Dolmetsch through the crowd. He had seen several pictures of Mike and knew he should be easy to spot. Now with hundreds of people walking everywhere it was not so easy.

"There he is!" cried Linda.

Don still could not see him but followed Linda's lead. Sure enough there he was indeed, with a woman by his side. Mike smiled and shook Don's hand. He introduced his girl-friend, Lilly, to them. Don knew she was from New York so English would not be a problem. Mike also spoke excellent English with just a trace of a Swiss accent. As they walked to the car Mike and Lilly told them of their plans for the day. Mike was obviously nervous and Don was as well. Don explained that it did not matter where they went as they were here to see Mike and Lilly not necessarily Switzerland or Zurich.

Lilly could see Mike and Don were both a bit nervous. Almost immediately she took charge. Soon they were on a whirlwind tour of the city of Zurich. She wanted this to go well for Mike and was determined to make it work. They took in the boat cruise on Lake Zurich and visited the world famous Grossman's Cathedral. They walked up and down the streets as Lilly described the significance of each place they visited.

At one point Mike smiled as he told them, "I am seeing things today I have never seen before and I have lived here all my life." Lilly was a typical New Yorker though and would never be accused of lacking energy or drive. Don wondered if any tour company could ever match her tour of Zurich.

Soon the two men began to relax and talk with each other. After a cup of coffee in a Starbucks coffee shop they returned to the car for the trip to Lilly's place. Mike explained that they would be staying there overnight.

"That's plan A," he said.

"What's plan B?" Don asked.

Mike grinned. "The same," he replied.

It sounded good to Don and Linda and they released any worries they had about finding a hotel to stay in. Don did not want to impose on Mike and Lilly but it seemed like a practical solution, so he let it go.

On the way to the house they stopped at Mike's former school and church. It was interesting for Don to see where and to hear how Mike had been raised. When they arrived at Lilly's place they relaxed for a while as Mike and Lilly made dinner reservations at a Swiss House Restaurant. As it turned out the place was almost fully booked for the evening however if they went right away they could get a place. Don and Linda had never been to this type of restaurant but looked forward to it. They parked just down the street and made the short stroll uphill to a normal looking house. Once inside it was obvious this was exactly what they had been told. It was a restaurant in a house run by the family that lived there. The place was packed, but they had kept a place for them near the entrance. Don and Linda listened to Mike and Lilly's explanation of the menu. Raised in a community of Swiss Mennonites back in Altona, Ontario, Canada, some of the menu items were familiar to

Don. He ordered what seemed a familiar name to him while Lilly, Mike and Linda ordered some of the more popular fare. The food was absolutely wonderful and by the end of the meal everyone was laughing and having a great time. After finishing the meal they drove back to Lilly's place. Mike brought out his files on the Dolmetsch family. Don also had his remaining copy of the Canadian family history.

Mike Dolmetsch, Don's Swiss cousin, stands in front of the church and school where he spent his school days.

"Do you know who Fritz Dollmatsch was?" Mike asked Don.

"Yes," said Don. "He was a famous cello player."

Mike was surprised. "How do you know about him?" he asked.

"I read about him in Der Stammfogle Der Familie Dolmetsch," Don said, referring to the family history in German that Martin Dolmetsch had sent him some seven months before.

"That's right," Mike said. "I have here a letter that he wrote to my grandfather just after the war, trying to find cello strings because they were in short supply in Germany. I also have a copy of the letter my grandfather wrote in reply." He handed the letters to Don. Although they were in German Don could understand many of the words, at least enough of them so as to get a sense of what the letters said.

"Man, I wish I had a copy of these," said Don.

"It shall be done," Mike said. "I will get copies made soon and will mail them to you."

Mike and Don had exchanged enough mail and info by now that Don knew his Swiss relative would come through on his commitment. As it turned out, his faith was well placed.

As the two distant cousins slowly went through the information they had there on the table they began to realize that they shared a similar passion for their Dolmetsch/Dulmage family. Although completely different personalities they got along extremely well. It was late in the evening before they finally decided to call it quits and turn in for the night. It wasn't until Don got into bed that he realized how tired he actually was. Soon everyone was sound asleep.

Don awoke the next morning to the sun streaming in the windows. Linda was already stirring. Slowly he rose and dressed to begin the day. As they looked out the window, toward the farm across the valley, Linda spied a small deer by the fence at the back of the house. Quietly, she hunted for her camera afraid that the deer would be gone before she could get a picture. The deer, however, appeared unconcerned. They took several pictures and were able to watch the animal for fifteen to twenty minutes. Used to seeing deer on their property back home in Canada they were pleased to have a visit from the Swiss variety. The deer here were smaller than what they saw back home but it was exciting just the same. Before long they heard stirring in the other part of the home. As they showered and dressed Lilly was busy making breakfast. Soon Mike appeared. He had been on the computer checking his e-mails.

"There was one there for you, Don," he said.

Don was surprised. He had given no one Mike's e-mail address.

"I wrote it down for you," Mike said, handing Don a small piece of paper. "It is from one of the cousins named Joachim Losch. He said if you are going to Sulz to call him first." Don looked at the paper. It said "Pfarrar Joachim Losch, Freudenstadt" with the phone number written underneath. He had not remembered saying anything to anyone about going to Sulz but it was their destination for the day. Later, they planned to return to the Park Hotel in Pforzheim where they had stayed the previous year. Don put the paper in his pocket and finished his breakfast. Lilly had done an excellent job. It was a North American style breakfast but with many of the popular German style foods.

Soon it was work time for both Mike and Lilly. Mike had told Don he would drop them at the train station on his way to work. Like everything on this trip it was about as perfect a plan as it could be. Mike parked the car and helped Don and Linda out with their suitcases.

"Will you be okay or should I go in with you?" he asked.

"We will be fine, Mike," Don said. "Thanks for everything, this has been a great visit."

Mike gave Linda a hug and shook Don's hand.

"Goodbye, cousin," Don said as they turned and walked into the train station. Mike waved goodbye and got into his car and drove off. It had been a great experience for all of them. Don hoped they would all meet again someday. Soon they found their way to the platform. The train was already waiting. Because it was a DB (Deutsche Bahn) train running from Germany it was easy to find with its distinctive German markings. There were not many on the train that morning and Don and Linda found a seat in a very similar location to the one they had used while coming in the day before. The scenery along the way was spectacular. Linda used the video camera as they rolled along. The train made all the same stops as it had the previous day. As it rolled through the countryside they passed the Swiss border into Germany. The falls on the river at Scheffenhausen were clearly visible from the train. Soon the land flattened out and they were rolling through farmland. Little villages stood along the tracks on the way. Sometimes the train would stop, other times it did not. Don hoped that Sulz would be one of the destinations but they flew right by the Sulz station without even slowing down. Don grabbed their luggage from the overhead rack.

"Let's go!" he said, as the train began to slow. He knew Horb would be the next stop. It seemed to take longer than he remembered to arrive at the Horb station. When the train stopped they stepped down into the bright sunlight. There were several buses parked neatly by the curb. Don and Linda tried to make some sense out of the signs. Meanwhile, several buses pulled away. Finally, Don asked one of the men, in a bus parked away from the depot, which bus went to Sulz. "Zwelf," (twelve) the man said, "in zwanzig minueten" (in twenty minutes).

In twenty minutes the same bus and driver pulled up to the number twelve stop. Don and Linda knew that sometimes the train ticket or in their particular case, the German rail-pass, covered some buses. He asked the driver and showed him their passes.

"Ich weiss nicht" (I know not), said the driver. "Eine moment" (one moment).

He took one of the passes and strode off into the ticket office. After about five minutes he returned.

"Nein" (no), he said shaking his head.

"Wie?" (how) asked Don. The driver looked around.

"Ohne" (without), he said softly, motioning them to board. Don understood that perfectly and wasted no time getting aboard. The driver motioned them to the rear of the bus and then summoned a couple of schoolboys to come with him. He asked Don and Linda why they were going to Sulz. The school children helped interpret between them.

"Mein Ahn war dort geboren" (my ancestor was there born).

"Ah, Vorfahr," came the reply.

Don had heard that before and understood it to mean forefather. He smiled and nodded. Soon the bus was loaded. The driver had told Don that they were "Die letzte" (the last) stop. By now the driver had figured out that if he kept the language simple and spoke slow that Don would understand. As he sat down in the drivers seat he explained to all the passengers who Don and Linda were and that they were from "Kanada hier kommen fuer Vorfahr suchen" (from Canada here coming for forefather searching). The passengers including several women and about eight or ten school children looked at them and smiled. It was obvious they all knew each other and the bus driver as well. The sense of community could be clearly felt. Having both been raised in small communities themselves, Don and Linda relaxed, as this was, for them, socially, at least, known territory. At each and every stop the bus driver came back and spoke to Don and Linda. He asked Don in German if he knew that the great American, General Schwarzkopf was a descendant of a Sulz family. Don had not known that even though he had read General Norman Schwarzkopf's book. That name would surface again a few days later but they did not know it at the moment. At the last stop before the Sulz depot the driver explained that they would be dropped off in the Marktplatz (Market square) as that would be the best place for them to find everything. He told Don that everyone would be looking at them and pointing "Da" (there). As they soon found out, that would be exactly the case. True to his word he pulled right up to the market square. As Don and Linda got off of the bus he tapped Don on the shoulder and pointed to a building across the street.

"Rathaus" (town hall), he said looking at Don to see if he understood.

"Ja, okay, " said Don nodding. "Vielen dank!" (thank you very much).

Don smiled as they stepped off the bus. Limousine service would have been a step below this. He could not ever remember being treated so well by any person involved in the transportation industry, ever! They sat down on the park bench for a minute as they tried to figure out what to do. Don thought he should phone this Pfarrar Joachim Losch.

"I think that is the man in the blue shirt that was at Martin's." Linda said.

"Do you think so?" Don asked. He was unsure. Now he wished he had asked. As he thought about it he didn't even know what this man wanted but it was the only lead he had for Sulz so he went over to the yellow pay phone to call. As he pulled the change from his pocket his heart sank. This phone only took phone cards, no money. He checked several others only to find the same result. After returning to the bench he told Linda what he had found.

"What are you going to do now?" she asked.

"I don't know." he replied. He sat down and thought it through as best he could. Finally they decided that Linda would watch the suitcases and Don would go to the Rathaus or town hall to see what he could find out. Once inside he was greeted by a young woman at the reception desk. He tried to explain in German what he wanted. He was making some headway but obviously not enough.

"Eine moment" (one minute), she said to Don. He was getting used to this expression. She started for the stairs and returned about three minutes later with a man about Don's age. He could speak some English and between the two languages they managed to communicate. Don showed him the note with Pfarrar Joachim Losch on it. The man seemed to know right away who that was.

"Pfarrar, preacher?" he said. "Aber Freudenstadt... umher forty-five minuten (but Freudenstadt... about forty-five minutes).

Don explained he needed a pay phone for "klein geld" (small change).

"Nicht hier," (not here), was the reply, "nur mit karte (only with card). Zu viel tieb" (too many thieves).

Don understood this. Obviously they had too many problems with people robbing the change boxes on the pay phones so they now only had phones that used phone cards. He took the paper from Don's hand and motioned Don to follow him upstairs. They went into his office and he picked up the phone and dialed the number. He handed Don the phone.

"Pfarrar Joachim Losch" the voice said on the other end.

"Don Dulmage hier von Kanada" (Don Dulmage here from Canada), and then he stopped. Speaking German was hard but for some reason on the phone it seemed at the moment impossible. His newfound helper took the phone and began to speak. It took a long time to convey what they needed to say. The man on the other end wanted to know if Don wanted him to come to Sulz. Don didn't know what to say. He had been just told to call if he went to Sulz. After a long and painful time the man in the office got it all straightened out. By this time Don was sweating profusely. Now he could hear the man giving directions of how to get to Sulz. As he hung up the phone he grinned at Don.

"All ist okay" (All is okay), he said. "Komm mit" (come with me).

He led Don through several offices in the upper floor of the building. Eventually they arrived at an open window. He spoke to Don in words only, not sentences, waiting each time to see if Don understood.

"Balcon?" (balcony) as he pointed to a balcony on a building across the street. "Unter, warten, okay?" (under, waiting).

Don understood and nodded. The man led him back through the offices and downstairs. He took Don to the town's information rack and motioned to Don to help himself to whatever he wanted. Don thanked him profusely and they shook hands and parted. He was astounded at the lengths this man had gone to help him.

"This is a great place to have your family come from," he thought. After helping himself to a few brochures he joined Linda in the market square. Don had noticed a Gasthaus (guest house) down the street from the Rathaus with the name Hecht on the wall. He believed Hecht might be the German version of the name Heck that was used in Ireland and North America. He was not completely sure, but decided to take a picture of the sign, just in case. By now they were very hungry. Don decided to see what he could find to eat. With the camera still hanging on his shoulder he set off down the street.

As he walked he saw a sign hanging over a doorway. The name was Kasper. He had seen a reference in one of the Canadian family trees to this name. He believed the spelling had been uncertain and it had said "Elisabeth Casper or Cosper." This spelling was close enough that he knew it would be the same family. He snapped a picture of the sign in case he needed it later, back in Canada. As he turned, he saw a store with an ice cream cone sign in the window. He knew he could handle this.

"Zwei eis bitte" (two ice creams, please), he said, "vanilla." The man nodded and proceeded to scope out the ice cream.

As Don paid he asked "Amerikaner?" (American).

"Nein, Kanadier" (no Canadian).

He was aware that everyone in the store was looking at him. He couldn't say he hadn't been warned. The bus driver had told them that, as visitors, everyone would be looking at them. The ice cream started to melt as he walked back to the bench where Linda sat with their luggage. He made it back okay and they sat there enjoying the cones. It was not a meal, but it would do for the time being. As they waited they talked about the trip so far.

In almost exactly twenty-five minutes they spotted a man coming toward them that they recognised from the reunion in Metzingen. It was the same man who had told Don "Donald Karl Dulmage, I am pleased to meet you." So this was Joachim Losch. Linda had been absolutely right. It all began to fit together for Don. This was Wolfgang Losch's (the family historian) younger brother Joachim. He was a retired minister and Don realized he would know his way around the churches and church records. First he motioned them to bring their suitcases to his green car. He stowed them in the trunk.

Don and Linda went to climb in but he said "Nein, Wir fussgangen" (no, we're walking). He walked out to the centre of the Marktplatz and looked around.

"Ah, Da!" (ah, there), he said pointing up at a church steeple high on the hillside. Soon they were climbing the steep streets to the church. It was obvious that he had not been here before but at least he seemed to know what he was looking for. Don realized had he tried this alone he would have had no idea what to look for. First, Joachim went to a large official looking house and rang the doorbell. He talked for a bit with someone and then turned and rejoined Don and Linda.

"Katholik" (Catholic), he said motioning toward the house where he had just been. He led them across the street to a smaller building and rang the buzzer. After a few words they were allowed inside. The entrance to the house was as it probably had been 400 years before. He made a large motion with his arm.

"Alt Dolmetsch haus" (old Dolmetsch house), he said.

"Ja?" (Yeah), said Don.

"Ja," was the reply.

After a few steps they entered a more modern section of the building and climbed the stairs to a large well-lit office. A younger woman met them at the doorway. He explained who he was and what they wanted. She smiled and led them down a hallway to a small room where there was a long table and an open cabinet at one end. In the cabinet were several volumes of very old and large books. Joachim spoke to her for a minute and she brought one of the volumes to the table. Joachim opened it to a certain page and there before them was a group of birth records for the Dolmetsch family. It took Don a minute or so to drink it all in. Here were the original records dating back to the 1700s for the town of Sulz. There were births clearly marked as well as other information. For some reason Joachim seemed to think this was the book Don wanted to see. Don knew his ancestor's father, if all was correct, was born here in 1640. This book was from the early 1700s. He knew his direct ancestor, Johann Adam Dolmetsch, would not be found in this book because his father (as near as they could tell) had not registered any of his children except for his firstborn who was his daughter. Don was a bit too excited at first and could feel himself getting warm. This was unbelievable to be able to see these records. He took a few minutes to compose himself and then gathered his nerve and asked the lady in German. "Ich moechte buch von eins, sechs, vier, null, sehen. (I want book from one, six, four, zero,[1640] to see). He was not sure he had said it right but she seemed to understand. Joachim seemed to think that was the wrong book and pointed to the one on the table.

"Nein" (no), said Don. "Nicht hier in Deutschland von

eins, seben, null, neune" (not here in Germany from one, seven, zero, nine [1709]). Don was too excited to even try putting the year dates together in the normal manner. The lady smiled and nodded. She bent down and got a book from the bottom shelf. Slowly she paged through it and then put her finger on a line and turned the book so they could all see. Don could hardly believe his eyes. There, in writing, entered in the year 1640, was the entry, "Dolmetsch... Joseph, 1640 geboren" (born).

That was exactly what his information had said and this was the town it had indicated. Everything seemed to check out. He sucked in his breath as the realization of what this actually was began to sink in. It was, for him, hard to believe these records still existed after all these years. He read as much as he could of the page. The lady was familiar with the Dolmetsch family name and seemed to be enjoying watching them as much as Don enjoyed seeing the records.

"Kann Ich foto machen?" (can I photo make), Don asked, knowing full well that normally photographing archives with a flash camera was often forbidden. She seemed to sense what he was thinking.

"Vom Kanada es ist okay" (from Canada it is okay), she said. She seemed to realize the importance of this and the long way they had travelled to find it. She held the book up so they could get a better picture. Don took several. After another good look he nodded and she closed the books and put them away. Joachim spoke to her for a few minutes. She then went to her office and returned with a key.

As they left, Don spoke to her.

"Vielen Dank" (thank-you very much), he said. "Entschuldigen, mein deutsch ist sehr schlecht" (excuse me, my German is very bad).

She smiled and waved aside his apology.

"She is a very nice woman," Don thought as they left the office and started down the stairs. Joachim led them through a different way and soon they were outside, standing in front of the old church. He took the key the woman had given him and opened the church door. Inside the church was beautiful. It was not a large church but everything was in perfect condition despite its obvious age. It was strange walking into this church. Both Joachim and Don knew this was the church of their mutual ancestors. Joachim was familiar with the items normally found in these old churches. He showed Don and Linda the old baptismal fount and explained that because the churches were unheated years ago, babies baptized in winter risked getting pneumonia and such. He went on to explain that that led to the practice of sprinkling, since it didn't pose such a health hazard. He then asked Don and Linda if they had both been baptized. Don confirmed that they had, but as adults by complete emersion. That seemed to surprise Joachim. Finally he pointed to the centre of Don's chest.

"Entaufen ist gut" (baptism is good), he said, "Aber ohne Jesus Christus in da (pointing to Don's chest) es machts nichts."(but without Jesus Christ in there it makes nothing).

Don wholeheartedly agreed. It was his belief as well as Joachim's that if a person did not accept Jesus Christ into their heart, all the baptisms and other rituals were meaningless. At once there was a new bond between these three believers. Don was thrilled to find that his family, even though separated between family lines for some 292 years, still held onto the faith that he had good reason to believe his ancestor Johann Adam Dolmetsch had held. Joachim seemed to sense it as well and from that moment on a stronger friendship developed between the two distant cousins. As they toured the church, Joachim, using a small history pamphlet that was in a rack at the back of the church, explained the history of the place and its relationship to the family. Don and Linda filmed his whole speech on video and would watch it over and over many times in the coming months. From that moment on, Don and Joachim seemed to have no trouble communicating. After locking up the church and returning the key, Joachim took Don and Linda to his car and motioned them to get in. He knew by now that they wanted to be in Pforzheim by nightfall, but it was still fairly early. He explained that he would take them to Freudenstadt where he lived and they could get a train from there to Pforzheim. Between Sulz and Freudenstadt lay the Black Forest or Schwarzwald. Joachim treated Don and Linda to a guided tour along the way. When they reached Freudenstadt he explained the history of the town and its planning to them. He took them to the market square and explained to them that this was the biggest Marktplatz in all of Germany. After waiting for Don and Linda to photograph the huge market square, he took them to his home.

Once inside his home Joachim offered Don and Linda something to drink as he and Don looked at the train schedule to see what would be the best route to take. His wife, Margarete, greeted them after a few minutes. She had been making strawberry jam and was at a stage in the process where she was unable to stop until finished. Don and Linda, both with a rural background, understood this completely and were not in anyway offended. In fact they were impressed to see their relatives on the other side of the ocean appreciated the joys of homemade foods as well.

They were also impressed that Margarete could speak such good English. They never did find out why. About this time Joachim discovered that the train left Freudenstadt for Pforzheim in about fifteen minutes. Quickly they said their goodbyes and made their way to the car. Joachim drove swiftly through the streets to the train station. The train pulled in just as they mounted the platform. As Don and Linda boarded the train and found their seats, Joachim motioned to some teenagers, on the train, to speak to him. Don was amazed at how the young people responded to Joachim and the respect he seemed to command from them.

"He is a credit to his profession as a pastor," Don thought. Although he didn't understand all that Joachim told the students, Don did realize that Joachim was making sure the students would look out for Don and Linda. Joachim seemed worried as he stood on the platform. Through the open window, Don spoke to him.

"Angst nicht! Wir sind Dolmetsch leute" (worry not; we are Dolmetsch/Dulmage people). Even Joachim who was normally a very staid individual could not suppress his grin. At that moment the train began to move and soon Joachim disappeared from view. Over the next year, whenever Don thought of Joachim he pictured him standing waving with that grin still on his face. It was a good memory and he would often reflect on it in the months to come.

They rode along for a half hour or so and stopped at very small station. Don and Linda were unsure what to do but while they were making up their minds one of the young teenage girls came and got them.

"That is the train for Pforzheim," she said in very good English, pointing to a single train car sitting directly in front of the station. Don was grateful that Joachim had asked these students to look out for them as he realized he would have otherwise been on the wrong train. This station, deep in the Black Forest, did not have many of the schedule boards and indicators that they had become used to in their visits to Germany. In fact this part of the system seemed to be totally run by young people. They made their way across the tracks and boarded the small train to Pforzheim.

The driver was a young man with a ponytail and a white shirt. He was a tall, young man and appeared to be friendly. Soon they were rolling along through the Black Forest. Don realized that from this small train they were seeing a part of this area rarely seen by tourists. Railcars of large, fresh-cut logs stood along the sidings. Despite the fact that they were very tired, the scenery held their interest. At one point the train slowed to a crawl as it passed over a trestle at least one hundred feet above the highway. It was hard to look at so Don distracted himself by looking at the inside of the car. After about an hour or so they saw a sign indicating Pforzheim was approaching. From this direction the appearance of the Pforzheim station was deceptive. It somehow seemed much smaller and hidden than it had been the previous year when they had arrived on a much larger train coming from the opposite direction. Once they stepped off of the train though Don felt right at home. He was now in "known territory" and they made their way quickly through the walkway under the tracks up into the station. It had been only a year and a week since they had been in this exact place before. As they walked through the station and out the front door Don spotted a taxi at the head of the line. Don approached the driver.

"Sind Sie frei?" (are you free), he asked. The driver nodded and loaded their suitcases into the trunk.

As they settled inside Don said, "Park Hotel, bitte" (Park Hotel, please).

The driver nodded and pulled away from the curb, taking the sharp turn that Don and Linda knew led to the road going to the Park Hotel. It was a very short drive to the hotel and after unloading the suitcases and paying the driver they headed for the revolving door. Once inside, Linda took the luggage to the side while Don went to the front desk.

"Ein zimmer, bitte, doppel" (a room, please, double), he said, as he placed his credit card on the counter. The young women seemed immediately to know he was English-speaking.

"Did you have a reservation?" she asked.

"No," Don replied. By this time she had picked up his credit card and typed in the name.

"Ah!" she said, "Mr. Don Dulmage from RR#1 Belleville, Ontario, Canada. I see you have stayed with us before. About a year ago I think."

"That's me," Don said. "I liked it so well here that I decided to come back."

While Don was just being friendly it was, in fact, true. Don and Linda had travelled extensively and stayed in many hotels and motels. The Park Hotel in Pforzheim was one of the very best they had ever visited. They had often spoken to each other of returning there.

The desk clerk handed Don the registration form, pointing with her pen to the rate for the evening. Don was pleased to see that it was substantially less than they had paid the previous year during the same time period. The desk clerk smiled.

"You are our regular customers now," she explained.

"Thank you," Don said. It pleased him to be treated so well after only his second visit. He hoped it would not be his last.

Don and Linda went up to their room and stowed their luggage. They freshened up and headed downstairs. The next day was their anniversary. They had now been married for thirty-one years. They knew they would not be able to celebrate the next day since Don had made arrangements to meet Michele (Mikala) Solimando. Michele was a direct descendant of Ludwig Dolmetsch who was the older brother of Don's probable ancestor, Joseph Dolmetsch. They had met over the Internet with the help of Reta Selleck. Don and Michele had made arrangements to meet in Pforzheim on June 6. Don was to phone Michele when he got there and had already tried once but was unsuccessful. Don and Linda decided to get something to eat. They realized that the last meal they had had was with Mike Dolmetsch and Lilly that morning in Zurich. Other than the ice cream cone in Sulz and the mineral water at Joachim's they had eaten nothing all day. It was hard to realize all that had happened since breakfast this morning. They knew from their visit here the previous year that the Park Hotel had a wonderful restaurant. The Maitre D seated them at a table by the window. Don ordered the meal in German. He was slowly becoming comfortable with it. Resigned to the fact that he might never be fluent he had learned that he could, at least, function in the language. Soon they were enjoying the asparagus/pork special that was featured this evening. They drank mineral water with their meal as well. Don had discovered his like of this while at Martin's and had since ordered it with every meal. Since they were both non-drinkers when it came to alcohol it was a reasonable substitute for the wine that was so popular with the German meals. Don had had to explain their desire not to drink any alcoholic beverages to his relatives. It had not been easy. He did not want, in any way, to offend them, but principles were principles and he knew if he could find the right words in his newly learned German language he would be able to help them understand. Since they were family and therefore would share similar thought patterns he reasoned that they would be able to accept his personal decision to avoid alcohol. He was right in that thought. Martin had sat down with him and asked for an explanation as it seemed the practice of not drinking wine, at least, was unheard of to them. Don had carefully explained that it was the practice in Canada as a result of his beliefs to abstain. He was also careful to explain that he realized in Europe that practice was unknown. Martin was very gracious and accepted the explanation. "I just wanted to know why," he had said in German. "It is okay."

Don reflected back on the visit as they ate. He had become very fond of these newfound relatives and hoped he would see them again.

Since it was their anniversary meal Don and Linda decided to try dessert.

"Wir moechten etwas nachtisch haben" (we want some desert to have), Don had told the waiter. "Ist das moeglich?" (is that possible).

The young waiter smiled and nodded. In a moment he reappeared with the dessert menus. Don and Linda ordered what looked like the German equivalent of a chocolate sundae. When the dessert arrived they were surprised at the size of it. Linda wondered if she would be able to eat it all, but then, considering it was their anniversary meal, decided to do her best. Don was already well into his by this time and no such thought ever crossed his mind. They had chosen well and both thoroughly enjoyed their desert. Linda got to wear a bit of hers as well when she pushed a little too hard with her spoon and it squirted up the straw at her. They both had a good laugh over that. All in all, it had been a very eventful day. It would be hard to ruin it at this point. They finished their meal and headed for their room. Don tried again to phone Michele. This time he was successful.

"Solimando," he heard.

"Dulmage here," he answered. Michele explained he was driving back from Zurich and should not be talking on the phone so they must keep it short. (It was illegal to drive and use a cell phone.) He agreed to meet them in the lobby of the hotel at 8 am the following morning.

"The perfect end to a perfect day," Don thought as he rolled into bed beside Linda. Minutes later he was fast asleep.

Breakfast at the Park Hotel was a real treat. Don had remembered this from the year before. All types of sliced cold meats with a variety of breads and buns were laid out before them. There were also several fruits and melon slices available as well as different types of German cereals. If there was ever a place to enjoy a traditional German style breakfast, this was it. Don and Linda made the most of it. It was still quite early when they finished eating. They had given themselves plenty of time to get ready for their meeting with Michele.

As they left the restaurant Linda suggested that Don settle up the bill while she finished packing the suitcases.

"I will bring them down," she said, "so you can wait for Michele in the lobby."

At first Don objected but then he realized the suitcases

were both very small so it would be, in reality, no real problem. As he paid the bill the desk clerk asked if he would also be coming back the next year.

"I hope so," Don said, not knowing if it would be so. "This is our favourite hotel worldwide."

As he turned to go he saw a young, dark-haired man looking at him from around the pillar in the lobby. The man smiled.

"Dolmetsch eyes?" he asked.

"Michele?" Don asked. Michele laughed and nodded. About that moment Linda came out of the elevator with the two suitcases and joined them.

"Come," said Michele. "I have brought my mother and my mother's car." His English was perfect. There was a slight trace of accent in his voice but it was just enough to add flavour. There would be no trouble understanding him. He led them to a small, white Fiat at the end of the parking lot. They loaded their bags and got in. Linda sat in the back with Michele's mother, Helga. Don sat in the front with Michele. Don knew that Michele's link to the Dolmetsch family was through his mother's side and speaking of Dolmetsch eyes he noticed she also had a bit of that family resemblance. Helga was very quiet and spoke mostly German although she seemed to understand some English. Don was glad Michele had brought his mom along. It seemed fitting that they would all be together today.

Michele announced that they would begin by visiting Leonberg, which was where the first records of "The Family Dolmetsch" existed. Don knew, from his e-mails with Michele, that this young man knew his family history. He expected that they would see a lot today but at this point he did not actually realize how much. As he drove, Michele told of his search for his ancestors and of how he had met Albrecht Dolmetsch just this year at a meeting of the Schonbein group that he belonged to. Now he was meeting Don and Linda. That meant that the descendants of all three Dolmetsch brothers from Sulz, Germany (Ludwig [Michele's] Joseph [Don's] and Zacharius [Martin's]) from the mid 1600s were now reunited. Don rolled these things over in his mind. It amazed him how all this had come to pass in just this one year. In fact, as he thought about the events that had transpired just in the last five days, he could scarcely believe they were real. Life was not normally like this. Things rarely worked out as planned but, so far, on this trip everything had exceeded his wildest dreams. He knew he would have trouble conveying the events of this week to his family and friends when he got back home. Why, he could scarcely believe them himself.

As they drove (somewhat aggressively) Helga occasionally cautioned Michele on his driving. Michele, like Don often was, seemed oblivious to the cautions and drove on. Don smiled to himself. Call them men or boys, it did not matter. When it came to cars and driving they were all the same the world over.

After about three-quarters of an hour they came down a long hill and into the town of Leonberg. Town was not really the right word. It was obviously a small city and construction was taking place everywhere. It had, in fact, grown so much since his last visit that Michele missed the turn to the old town centre or Marktplatz. He hoped his Canadian cousin was not upset. He glanced at Don as he drove. Don was a large man, bigger than Michele had imagined, but he seemed totally unconcerned as Michele made his way through the streets desperately trying to find the right one. "Maybe he doesn't care," Michele thought but dismissed the idea right away. "If he did not care then he would not have come several thousand kilometres to be here," he reasoned.

Don was determined to be a gracious guest. He was well aware of how things sometimes went askew as one tried to make them perfect. He was confident that Michele knew what he was doing and one little misstep here or there was certainly not going to ruin their day. He noticed Michele glancing over at him and hoped he was not putting his new-found relative under undue pressure. Soon Michele found the street he was looking for and they parked the car. They were downtown, just a stone's throw from the market square (Marktplatz). Don and Linda were amazed as they walked into the market area. It was just as it would have been some 600 years previous, save for the odd car parked along the street. There was music playing and a soft rain fell as they walked. It was like stepping back in time.

Michele gave them a good tour of the old town. Their common ancestor, Konrad Dolmetsch had once been the mayor or head man in this town and some of the buildings, including a large palace dated from that era and his time in office, were still here. Michele took them to a church where it is known Konrad Dolmetsch attended and they all sat in the mayor's seat together. Michele told them one could say, with reasonable accuracy, that it was the same seat Konrad sat in, in the 1400s and it is still, to this very day, the mayor's seat in that church. Michele told Don that he had a book for him on the town of Leonberg that he would give him later. After completing the visit to Leonberg, Michele drove them to the nearby town of Hofingen (pronounced Hurfingen). Here he took them to the Protestant church. An organist was practising while they were there and it only added to the experience. It amazed Don that even in a small church like this there was a full-fledged pipe organ. They met a man and his wife near the rear of the church who appeared to be the caretakers. As Michele spoke to him Don realized this language was different from what he had learned. Not that he expected to understand everything, but he did expect to understand more than he could hear. Michele explained that the man spoke the Swabish dialect of German and it was somewhat different than the standard Schreib Deutsch (literally written German) Don had learned. Don knew that the family were Schwabisch people. In fact, Reta Selleck had first told him that the previous year. He was not aware, however, that the language was different. Michele explained that many of the older people still preferred to speak the Schwabish dialect. He had no trouble with it since he was raised nearby and spoke it as well. Next, they visited the local museum for the town. The door was open so they went up the stairs. On the way up Michele pointed to a photo on the wall. Don recognised it from a newspaper photo Michele had sent him. It was known as "Der Spitelhof" and was an old Dolmetsch family home that just a year previous had succumbed to the ravages of time and had to be torn down. Later, Michele was to show them where it had been located. As they entered the museum on the second floor they found several people working away. A lady, who was obviously in charge, came over and announced that they were only working, the museum was not actually open. Michele was not so easily put off and explained to the lady that he was here with a Dolmetsch descendent from Canada. The Dolmetsch family had lived in Hofingen at one time and he mentioned a couple of specific names. It seemed to strike a chord with this woman and she nodded and smiled. She held up her hand indicating for them to wait, then turned and hurried up a flight of stairs. Seconds later she returned with a hard cover book still in its wrapping. She handed it to Michele and he gave it to Don.

"This is for you," he said.

"How come?" Don asked.

"It does not matter, how come," Michele said. "Maybe because I spoke to her in Schwabish," and then he laughed. Don was mystified. He knew the book was easily worth thirty or forty dollars Canadian. Just to have someone give you one like that was unbelievable.

"You will find some Dolmetsch people in there," Michele told him. As Don thanked the lady she just nodded and smiled. Minutes later they were back in the street, returning to the car. It was now getting close to noon. Don could tell without checking his watch because he was getting hungry.

Next, they drove to the town of Asperg. Don knew that was where Michele and his family lived. They drove down a street to a white, two-storey house and parked in front. In the driveway was a red Porsche. Don recognised it from photos Michele had sent him, as Michele's own car. They took a short break here then headed uptown on foot. Michele announced they were going for dinner at a typical Schwabish restaurant. Don and Linda already knew a bit about Schwabish food. Sigi Schwienbacher had taught them to make a special type of Schwabish pasta called spaetzle when he had visited with Mike in February. His wife had sent along a special little spaetzle machine for them and a written recipe. They had made it often and had grown fond of it. Sigi had told them it was "real Dolmetsch food."

Secretly, Don hoped it would be on the menu here as he wanted to see if it tasted anything like what they had learned to make back home. The restaurant was an open-air type set under a canopy in the courtyard. The waiter, who Don assumed was also the owner, was dressed in old style Schwabish clothes and was a very gracious man. He seated them and talked with Helga and Michele. Obviously, they knew him well. Don and Linda looked over the menu. Sure enough, there it was spaetzle und rhindefleisch (spaetzle and beef). Don and Linda decided immediately to order that.

"Do you know what that is?" Michele asked. Don told him the story of Sigi and Mike and learning to make spaetzle.

"Okay," said Michele. "I just wanted to be sure."

The meal came fairly quickly. Don and Linda could not have ordered better. The meat was done to perfection and much to their amazement the spaetzle tasted almost exactly like their own homemade meal in Canada. Don looked at Linda.

"We must have been doing it right," he said with a grin. Linda smiled and nodded. It did truly taste almost exactly the same.

As they finished their meal, Helga reached in her bag for her camera. Linda immediately did the same. Almost out of nowhere the waiter appeared and offered to take their pictures. That pleased everyone because now they would all be in the photos. He was not haphazard about it either, but went to great lengths to get them both good pictures from the right angle. Don was beginning to like this fellow already. He could not seem to do enough for them.

"What's next?" Don asked.

"Markgroningen," said Michele as he finished his dessert. "You will like it there."

When they finished the meal they walked back up the street to the Solimando home.

After a few minutes inside they all returned to the car and set out for Markgroningen. Markgroningen had been prominent in the Dolmetsch family history. Don had already read about it in the old Stammfolge Der Familie Dolmetsch that Martin had sent him. In fact, he had even been to the city's web site and had printed out an aerial photo of the town. It was exciting to realize that in just a few short minutes they would actually be there. Michele parked the white Fiat in a parking lot near the edge of the Marktplatz and they walked toward the centre of town. Even outside the Marktplatz one could tell some of these buildings were very, very old. When they entered the market area, one of the first buildings they stopped at was known as the Wimpeln Haus. It was built by Elisabeth Dolmetsch who had married into the Wimpeln family in the 1400s. The building stood at one corner of the Marktplatz and extended almost halfway down the one side. Workmen and scaffolding were everywhere. The front of the building was boarded up with fresh plywood while workmen worked away. In one area they were removing some of the old damaged material while in another a new freshly repaired wall was taking shape. Michele stepped through the opening and looked around to see who was in charge. He quickly found the man who appeared to be giving the orders and explained that they were all descendants of the Dolmetsch family. He even let it slip that the two of them had come all the way from Canada to see this place. The foreman seemed to understand and gave them permission to walk through the old home. Don was surprised at this. In Canada it would have been a lot more difficult and there would have been the mandatory hard hat and safety shoes to wear. Here it seemed a lot simpler. As they explored the old home Don thought about just how smoothly everything had gone. He had watched Michele throughout the day. He had realized that his distant cousin had a very pleasant way about him that was very disarming. He reasoned this had to be a major factor in allowing them to see as much as they had. People just seemed to automatically like Michele. He was in fact just exactly that, a very likable person.

As they strolled through the restoration site, Don was also surprised at Michele's knowledge of early German history. Although he had degrees in both electrical engineering and computer engineering, Don couldn't help wonder if Michele hadn't missed his calling. He mentioned it as they left the building.

"Maybe you should have been a high school history teacher," Don told him. "You seem to know an awful lot about it and you certainly know how to make it interesting." Don's comment was met with nothing more than a smile and shrug. They walked on up the street. Michele took them to a building in the centre of one side of the town square or Marktplatz.

They walked all around the building. Michele explained to Don and Linda that this house was an old Dolmetsch home. Although the people currently living here no longer carried the Dolmetsch name they were nevertheless Dolmetsch descendants through one of the Dolmetsch daughters. He went on to explain that this house had never been sold but had remained within the family, handed down from one generation to the next, for over 500 years. It was mind boggling, to say the least, to stand in the town square and look at this building, realizing that Michele, his mother, Helga and Don all carried the same blood line as the people who still dwelt in that home. Don was amazed at all he had learned from Michele. To find one's ancestral relatives was one thing, but to find the place where your family name first surfaced and was once a major part of this city's life was more that Don could ever have hoped for. To stand in front of a family home 500 years later and to realize the people living there still, were actually your relatives, was hard to comprehend. Michele made several attempts to visit that old Dolmetsch home while they were in Markgroningen. The owner of the home was not there at the time, although he was scheduled to return later that day. Despite several phone calls they never did find him at home. In one last attempt Michele summoned all his nerve and asked the man's secretary if it would be possible to have, at least, a peek inside. It was not to be. Michele was visibly disappointed, but Don figured if Michele could not charm his way into the home, then it could not be done by anyone.

While in the market square in a store right next to the old Dolmetsch home, Linda saw on display a hand carved, wooden nativity set in the window. With a little encouragement from Don she decided to investigate. Helga spoke to the lady who owned the shop as they entered. Surprisingly the woman spoke excellent English and was able to talk easily with Linda. To be sure the set was not inexpensive, but it was unique. Linda looked at Don.

"Buy it now" Don said. "You will never have another chance." Linda felt a bit guilty as the lady carefully wrapped and packed each piece, but Don encouraged her. He was also interested in the set as it was from a town that had played a high spot in his family's history and besides it was very well made so at least you knew you were getting your money's worth.

From here they went to the Protestant church. It had been locked when they first went there so they had gone to the Catholic church to look around. This time the church was open. The organist was seated high up in the organ loft. The huge, old stone building rang with the sound of the classical style hymns as she practised for the next Sunday's service.

The old pipe organ was a real treat to hear and this organist obviously knew how to play it. Don could see her watching them in a mirror she had sitting beside the music book on the organ.

They spent quite a bit of time in the old church. Michele said the family would have attended this very building. Don had seen in the old Stammfogle Der Familie Dolmetsch the story of how and when the family first became Protestants so he knew Michele was probably absolutely right in saying this. The old book had gone so far as to say that when Martin Luther nailed his thesis to the church door, a Dolmetsch man, who had been choirmaster and secretary, left the Catholic church and there had been no Catholic Dolmetsches ever since. Don had smiled when he read that as he knew of at least two from his own family who were Catholics by marriage and he was sure that there were probably others. Still, the absoluteness of the statement appealed to him. One thing was for sure, many branches of this family still held onto their strong Christian beliefs.

From the church they went back to the market square for some refreshments. Don ordered slowly in German and asked the waitress for the bill when they were done. She immediately switched to English.

"My German must be terrible," Don thought. She did not ask him what he had said, though, so he began to relax a bit.

"At least she understood," he told himself. "It could have been worse."

From here they went by car to the old fort high on a hill in the town of Asperg. The old fort was now a prison hospital. It was, in fact, the very place where tennis player Stephie Graf's father was held during his imprisonment for "creative" bookkeeping. The fort reminded Don of Old Fort Henry back home in Canada. The layout of the two places was so similar Don wondered if they were designed by the same person. The view from the fort was wonderful. One could see Stuttgart off in the distance as well as all of the towns they had been to that day.

From here they went to the town of Ludwigsburg. While Don and Linda strolled the town square with Michele, Helga did a bit of quick shopping. The next stop was the Palace of Ludwigsburg. With its grand walls and millions of flowers, it was a sight worth seeing. Don and Linda were getting a little tired at this point but ignored it, for the most part, as Michele and Helga showed them around one of their favourite spots. There was really enough to see here that one could have easily spent the whole day touring it. It was getting late when they finished. It had been a full day and they drove back to Asperg in silence. Michele showed them around his parents' house and his mother's garden. It was truly beautiful and one could easily tell Helga loved her garden. Don was especially impressed by Helga's lemon tree sitting in a huge pot in the garden. Michele explained his father had made his mother a "winter garden" as they called it in the south side of the garage and they put the lemon tree in there in the fall. That kept it warm all winter and then in the spring it was returned to the garden. It obviously worked well as the tree was heavy with ripe lemons. Don wondered if it would work at home in Canada. He knew it got colder at home than here in Asperg, but even here it was far from a tropical climate. Some day he would have to try it. That was for sure.

Later that evening they sat around the kitchen table eating a light supper. The German people ate much differently than Canadians. Don figured that it must have had some merit too as he had not seen one seriously overweight person since arriving in Germany. These people had their big meal of the day at noon. Supper was more like a snack for them. The food was good though. The fresh crusty rolls and cold meats with a good selection of cheese seemed to be all one needed. They also had huge Schwabish pretzels that in reality tasted more like donuts. Don had to restrain himself from eating too many. As they talked, Helga would get Michele to translate. Michele could tell that although not fluent Don could understand much of what his Mother had said. At one point he told her just that.

"Momma, he understands you." She looked at Don and he nodded. Using both English and German they talked late into the night. Michele gave Don two more books. One was the history of Leonberg and the other was a book on Markgroningen much of which was written by another Dolmetsch descendant, Hilde Fendrich. He also had photocopied the Stammfolge der Family Dolmetsch. Don now had three copies of this book already and so he told Michele that. Later he wished he had just taken it and said thanks. He did not want to hurt his newfound cousin's feelings. Finally it came time to go to bed. Helga showed Don and Linda where they would be sleeping and they got ready for a good night's rest. Michele knocked on the door a few minutes later and asked Don to meet him in the hall. Don grabbed his shirt and stepped to the hall. Michele explained that they had not properly said goodbye. He had to return to work in Zurich by the next morning and so would be leaving around 5 am to allow himself time for the drive. Don thanked Michele for everything. He invited him to come, with his family, to Canada for a visit and said he hoped they would be able to meet again. Early that morning Don heard the soft rumble of the powerful, vintage Porsche as it slipped out the driveway and off into the darkness heading for Switzerland. He had grown very fond of his cousin in the one day they had spent together and wished him nothing but the best. Most of all he hoped they would someday meet again. Don drifted back to sleep only to waken a couple of hours later to the sound of birds singing. It was light now. Linda stirred and they whispered for a few moments. They decided to get up and get dressed. While Don shaved, Linda packed the suitcases. They made sure they had everything then headed downstairs. Nobody was around so they sat down at the table. Moments later Helga returned. She had been to the bakers for some fresh buns for breakfast.

"These people really know how to live," Don thought. No one would go out for baked goods that early at home. In fact there would be no place open that early, but here it seemed normal. As they ate they talked back and forth. Don and Helga made a pact. She would e-mail Don regularly in Deutsch (German) if he would always reply in English. Don agreed. Helga seemed, to him, to be very shy but he hoped she would keep in contact. As it turned out she was true to her word and the two distant cousins e-mailed each other on a regular basis over the next year. After a good German style breakfast they loaded the suitcases in the car and Helga drove them to the train station. Their train was already sitting in the station and Helga insisted on bringing Linda's suitcase to the platform. Linda and Helga said their goodbyes then Helga turned to Don. Don grasped her by the shoulders and leaned over and whispered in her ear.

"Goodbye dear cousin." She said nothing as he turned and boarded the train. They could see her standing on the platform as they waited for the train to leave. She waved as it began to move. Don was certain he had seen what looked like a tear in her eye as they left. He could understand it too. Despite the fact that their family had been separated some 292 years, there was still an unexplainable bond between them. It was hard to believe, but it was there all the same.

Before long they were rolling through the countryside heading for Mainz and their second cruise down the Rhine. They had a lot to think about from the events of the past few days. Now on their own again, it was good to reflect on the time they had spent with the various members of the old family. So far, this trip had turned out to be beyond what Don could ever have hoped for. What lay ahead, he did not know, but if nothing else worked out they already had experienced many things that few people ever get to enjoy. There was so much to think about that the actual train ride was just a blur. For a long time they rode along in silence, each lost in their own thoughts. Somewhere they changed trains, but Don scarcely remembered it as he reflected on the week that had passed. Although they had been in Germany just seven days, it seemed like a month or more. As the train pulled into the Mainz station Don was jolted back to the present. They made their way through the train station and out into the street. The station was still being restored but

141

tremendous progress had been made since the previous year. One could easily envision the finished project from across the street. There was no question as to where they would stay. It would be the Central Hotel that they had stayed in the previous year. Don walked up to the desk and asked for a room. When he presented his credit card the woman at the desk said,

"I see you were here with us last year."

"We were," Don replied. "Maybe we will make it every year."

"That would be good," the woman said as she pointed on the registration form where she wanted him to sign. Don glanced at the price and noticed again that he had received a substantial discount over the previous year's lodging. They were on the same floor this year but in a different room. It was still early in the day so the desk clerk asked for some time to prepare the room. Don asked if she could keep their suitcases there while they explored the city. She assured him it was no problem.

Mainz was a place they had visited before. They had a good idea of how to get around and so they set off on a stroll downtown. Their favourite spot was near the Marktplatz by the Gutenberg Museum. There was a large rose garden in Mainz on the way to the Marktplatz so they took time to walk through it as they headed to the downtown core. It was a leisurely stroll and they visited several of the shops along the way. Don was always poking around the bookstores. This time he found several to visit but nothing in particular caught his eye. Linda found a luggage store and spent time looking for a small case to put their extra things in. They were carrying more than they had room for, thanks to the generosity of their relatives and friends so they needed another small bag to hold the extra things. She found one she liked and showed it to Don. He took it to the clerk and conducted the transaction in German. Soon they were back in the street looking for a place to eat. They found a really interesting place on the corner. It had baked goods on display in the front window and a large attractive restaurant in the rear. They decided to eat there. The food was to their liking and Don was able to conduct the whole ordering and paying process in German. Mike Schwienbacher had told him he knew enough vocabulary to get by. He remembered Mike saying, "You just need to be thrown into the German swimming pool and you will soon learn how to swim." Obviously Mike knew what he was talking about. Don mimicked Mike's style. He spoke slowly and did not allow himself to panic or to be rushed. He was surprised how well it worked. It pleased him to be able to function in the language of his ancestors. Still it surprised him that he could. They spent the rest of the day walking the streets and visiting the many shops. It was good to spend the time together. It had been awhile since they had had much time alone. They ate supper at a Wienerwald Restaurant. Mike Schwienbacher had told Don about them when he was in Canada. He said they were sort of a German version of the Canadian, Swiss Chalet restaurants. That proved to be a fairly accurate description. The menu said "Kicky Chicken." It was just as advertised. Chicken, with a bit of extra spice. After buying some stamps and post cards they returned to their hotel, rescued their suitcases from the lobby and headed for their room. The one thing they had remembered about this hotel was the old, tiny elevator. It was about the size of a phone booth but advertised room for five "personnen."

"They would have to be leprechauns," Don had said

because obviously five normal sized people would not fit in this elevator. They took the time to videotape it as they wanted to show their friends back home that it really was as small as they had said. Before long they were in bed and sound asleep. They awoke the next morning to the noises of construction across the street. Don was grateful to be awakened since they had to be at the Rhine cruise kiosk by 8 am. They showered and packed then headed down for breakfast. Breakfast was served in a room in the rear of the hotel. They remembered it from the year before. They took time for a second cup of coffee before they set out for the day. The procedure was exactly the same as last year. After paying the bill Don flagged a cab for the ride to the dock on the Rhine. The driver asked if they were Canadian and told them he had relatives in London, Ontario. Don paid the man then they headed for the kiosk. The previous year they had only gone as far as Koblenz but this year they planned to go all the way to Koln (Cologne). They got their tickets and boarded the boat. Since they were among the first to board they had their choice of seats. They found a table in the forward restaurant towards the corner of the boat. It was the perfect spot. Their small suitcases fit between the table and the wall just perfectly and they could see both forward and out of the one side. Within fifteen minutes the boat filled up with people and was underway. Their waitress was a tall German woman in her mid-forties. Don was able to conduct everything for the whole trip in German. He wasn't quite sure if his German was that good or her understanding exceptional. In the final analysis he guessed it didn't matter. It was good to get the practice no matter what the case might be. The trip was interesting, but relatively uneventful. Near the end of the day about 50 kilometres from Cologne a party of about thirty people joined the boat for the final leg of the journey. One of their members was the spitting image of Norman Schwarzkopf, the great American, Gulf War General. He looked so much like him that Don wondered if it could actually be him. As it turned out it wasn't but the resemblance was uncanny. They arrived in Cologne near dusk. Finding a hotel proved difficult. Some were too expensive. (Don figured that over 300DM was too much to pay.) Finally he found one that had no rooms available, but they also owned a suite-type hotel further up the street. They phoned ahead and made Don a reservation. He could relax a bit now as the pressure was off to find a place to stay. Cologne was a busy spot at night and it was crowded enough that just walking the streets was a challenge with so many people around. Eventually they found their place and checked in, then headed for their room. They spent some time watching TV then drifted off to sleep. The next morning they awoke a bit later than usual. They had no particular schedule to keep so they took their time showering and getting ready. During breakfast they discussed their plans. They had wanted if possible to continue to Holland by boat, but that was becoming a bit too complicated to figure out. Since the train more or less followed the Rhine river anyway they had decided that would be the most practical route. Don was not feeling all that well this day. Why, he didn't know. It wasn't that he was sick he just didn't have his usual spark. They left the hotel and walked toward the huge Cologne Cathedral. It was much bigger and more ornate than one would realize from looking at photos. They decided to go inside. The sheer magnificence of the building was astounding. They spent almost an hour walking around and taking pictures. Don was interested in seeing what literature they had on display. It was much more interesting than he had imagined. After a while they decided to continue on their journey. The train station was close by the cathedral. That, they had learned from the city map they had purchased. After climbing a spiral staircase up over the roadway they found themselves at the Cologne train station. Linda went into the station to find some coffee and some water to drink while Don rested for a bit on the benches near the platform. After a cup of coffee they decided to check the schedule. They found the train on the posted schedule but Don was unsure if their passes would be good into Holland. He went to the ticket window and asked. As it turned out, they were good into Holland till the first stop. After that they would need new tickets. The saleswoman told him he could buy them right there. That suited Don.

"Fuer Hoek van Holland," he said. She nodded and processed the tickets. The transaction took only seconds and he felt much better now knowing they could at least get to the north end of Holland without any trouble. When they boarded the train they found a seat near the middle of the car. From there they had a good view in both directions. It did not take all that long to leave Germany behind and head into Holland. They were amazed at the sudden change in the countryside. Holland was very flat, much flatter than either of them had imagined. Out the window they could see many farms along the way. In the fields were the Holstein cows that were so popular in Canada as well.

Eventually the train pulled into the station and they had to switch from the DB train to the Dutch one. From Deutsch to Dutch as it were. Don had had numerous discussions with people back home who said they were Pennsylvania Dutch and so thought they were from Holland originally. When he tried to explain to them that it meant Pennsylvania "Deutsch" which was really German, they would often shrug in disbelief. He never understood that, as the fact had been well taught in Canadian grade school history but somehow many people seemed to have forgotten. Now here it was as plain as the nose on your face: from the German rail system known as the Deutsche Bahn, or DB for short, to the Dutch rail system in Holland. He wished some of those disbelievers were with him right then. As they changed trains they noticed quite a difference in the two trains. The German ones were fast and very modern. The Dutch train, while there was nothing wrong with it, appeared a bit more conventional. Soon they were on the move again. They passed through several towns along the way. The houses were all in neat little rows and seemed very similar. They looked more like the older homes in Canada than the German houses they had seen during the past week. In fact, Holland in general reminded Don of Canada. He could see why so many from there had found Canada a good place to live in. It was very similar in appearance. Now and then they would catch a glimpse of the Rhine as it wound its way through Holland to the sea. Eventually they began to see the dykes. As they neared the end of their journey they realized the ships alongside the railway were actually floating on waterways that were at a higher level than the railway tracks. It seemed strange. They had been told, even as children, of how Holland had reclaimed much of the land in the north from the sea, but to see it for real was a bit unnerving. Don thought back to the story in their old grade school reader about how a young Dutch boy had saved Holland from flooding by holding his finger in a hole in the dyke to stop the water flow. No one seemed to know if the story was true, but he could not help thinking about it now.

The train stopped in Rotterdam and then moved on to the end of the line in an area known as the "Hoek van Holland" or the Hook of Holland. It was right at the sea and from here boats sailed on a regular basis to England and beyond. Don was fairly sure this is how his ancestor Johann Adam Dolmetsch had sailed from this general area. He wasn't sure how they would get to England or where they would stay before leaving by ship the next day. As it was, it was decided for them. They followed a group of women off the train. A large ferry could be seen to the left of the train sitting at the dock. They decided to follow the ladies over to the building in front of the ferryboat. It turned out to be the ferryboat terminal. Don checked when the next ferry left for England and was told in three hours. He could not believe their good fortune and immediately purchased two tickets for walk-ons. As they waited in the terminal they realized they were hungry. There was a small restaurant, or rather snack bar, in the building. Don checked the menu but saw no credit card signs. He asked the man at the counter if they took credit cards but was told no. To be honest, it did not surprise him. He had many Dutch friends back home and he knew when it came to money they took it very, very seriously. He had often teased them about it, but secretly admired their indisputable ability to stretch a dollar. He learned long ago that although some-times their methods didn't make sense to him the results spoke for themselves. He smiled as he thought about it. "Cash" that was what they liked. Unfortunately he and

Linda had no Dutch money. They had not needed any since they had bought their tickets in Cologne and had made no stops along the way other than to change trains. Don explained it to the man. He asked what type of money they had. Don told him they had some Deutsch marks (German money). He agreed to sell them some sandwiches for Deutsch marks but specified the price range. He said he could always get rid of a few DM but not too many. That was okay with Don and they found a table and purchased their food. It tasted good. He had forgotten how hungry he was. They had had little since breakfast except for some cookies Linda had bought that morning. Don paced the floor after they ate. He was anxious to get going. Waiting was always hard, but today it seemed worse than usual. English was no problem for the Dutch people. He had been told they all learned it and this particular town, whose whole existence depended on trade with England, was well versed in their neighbouring country's language. He had to admit it was a relief to hear it again. It surprised him that he felt that way.

After what seemed to be an eternity, they were allowed to board the ferry. It was a positively huge ship and had several restaurants and bars on board. They found a seat near a window and settled in. Their luggage had been checked just like at an airport so they were free to roam around. Once the boat began to move out to sea Don left the seat and walked up toward the bow. As he looked up he saw a faded map in a picture frame overhead. It said under the map it was the typical route taken by ships in the 1700s travelling from this area of Holland to England. Knowing this was probably the exact route taken by the ship Batchelor that had brought the Dolmetsch family from

Holland to England in 1709, Don took out his camera and snapped a picture. He knew it would not be a very good one but he also realized he would not likely ever get another chance. Awhile later they went up into one of the onboard restaurants for a dinner buffet. The food was good and more like they were used to in Canada. They took their time eating and thoroughly enjoyed their meal. It was expensive, but for some reason he didn't care. They had been away from home for about ten days now and in a different, but agreeable culture, still, this familiar food and language pleased him. As he reflected on it he realized that the last few days had been fairly stressful, even though they had thoroughly enjoyed them.

The trip across to England was not long. The ferry was a highspeed version and travelled at an average speed of fifty-five knots. Soon they could see land ahead, as well as many ships on all sides of them. Harwich, England was obviously a busy port. It seemed to take forever as the ferry wound its way into the port and then eventually to its dock. Finally the announcement came that it was time to disembark. As they walked down the passenger ramp they were aware of a lot of yelling going on behind them. Several young Englishmen, in their late teens and early twenties, had been on a trip to the seedy side of Holland. Now drunk to their limits on whiskey and beer, they were shouting the sordid details of their trip to the whole world. In spite of the mixed crowd around them they made no attempt to restrain themselves in either language or details. This was one part of British life that Don and Linda could have lived without. A security guard followed close behind, but wisely only engaged them in conversation as he made numerous calls on his cell phone. He was aware that he would be no match for them on his own. Some boarded the train and were gone, but several headed for the parking lot and a parked car. Before they could get their things loaded into their car, a police car drove up and took charge of the situation. Don never did find out what had happened. He now had troubles of his own. After standing in line at the train ticket window for some twenty minutes it was finally Don's turn. Their plan was to cross England by train from Harwich to Holyhead and then take the ferry for Ireland. They had planned to spend the night there. Linda had suggested to Don that that might work in Germany but England and Ireland would be different. Don had not listened. He had reasoned that out of sheer pride, if nothing else, the British would make sure their rail system was up to standards. After all, every "Brit" he had ever met had taken every opportunity to tell Don how, in Britain, "this was better and that was better." While he had taken that with a grain of salt he thought their systems would be at least at a competitive standard. He was about to learn just how wrong he could be.

"May I help you Sir?" the man in the ticket window asked. Don cringed. How he hated that accent. He tried to ignore it. "How do I get from here to Holyhead?" he asked.

"Oh, You don't want to go there!" the man said.

"Oh yes I do," Don replied. He was beginning to feel a bit warm.

"Oh no you don't," the man said. Don was almost over the edge. His voice was loud and firm as he spoke.

"Look!" he said, "I didn't ask you if I wanted to go there. I asked you how do I get there. Your opinion is of little interest to me!" He remembered how annoying he thought these people had been when they came to Canada in the fifties and sixties, seemingly scooping up all the government jobs and carrying on with an air of superiority. Often they had referred to Canada as a colony. They had annoyed Don then, but this man was really getting to him now.

"That would take three and a half to four hours," the ticket man said. "You don't want to do that."

"I don't care if it takes three weeks!" Don replied. "I just want to know how to get there." He stared at the round hole in the ticket window glass and wondered if he could pull that man's little round, bald, empty head through the hole. It had been years and years since he had allowed himself to be this upset. At about that moment, a small, pleasantly dressed English lady touched him on the arm.

"He is not going to tell you," she said. "Come over here and I will help you." She led him over to where Linda was standing and explained that the trains in England did not run like the ones in Germany. In fact, there would be no train to Holyhead tonight. The only reasonable option was to take the shuttle train into London and get a hotel. Tomorrow it would be easier from the London train station. Linda looked at Don. She had tried to tell him it would be harder here, but he wouldn't listen. Often the very thing that had given him success in life, his determination, also caused him grief when it returned in the form of stubbornness. Linda had been a bit worried as she watched him at the window. She could tell he was getting steamed. She wasn't really worried he would do anything physical, but she knew he had a sharp tongue and would use it, without hesitation, to cut any unsuspecting person, who challenged him, down to size. She hadn't heard all of what was going on but was relieved when this lady took Don aside. Don nodded and thanked the lady. He took a few minutes to calm down and then he discussed it with Linda. They decided that was probably their best option. To be truthful, at this point, it was their only option. Don returned to the ticket window.

"Two for London," he said and pushed his credit card through the opening. As the man processed the card and the tickets he talked on and on about how right he was. Don had already realized this was someone he could not get along with and had turned his selective hearing to the "off" position. Nothing, absolutely nothing, this idiot might have to say was of any interest to him. He signed the slip and took his tickets. Together they headed for the train.

The train was a far cry from what they had grown accustomed to. It was old, dirty and somewhat banged up. It seemed like every screw in it was loose and rattling. They stared out the window as the train clattered along.

"This must be some of the same scenery Johann Adam Dolmetsch saw as they came to the Blackheath refugee camps near London way back in 1709," Don thought. Much of the English countryside appeared untouched. Don was not sure if Johann Adam had come this exact route, but it would have been, at least, similar. The train seemed slow and the trip seemed to take forever.

Finally after a series of bridges and tunnels the train slowed to a stop in the Liverpool Station. Liverpool Station was very modern and bright. It was as if one had stepped into another world. It was a busy place, too, and people were rushing everywhere. Don and Linda walked to the centre of the mezzanine and took a few moments to get their bearings. It was hard to figure out which way to go. Don remembered the lady at the first station had told them there was a nice hotel by the station that often had good weekend rates. Don and Linda had been so many places and seen so much that they had lost track of time. It was a bit of a shock to realize that it was the weekend. They walked outside the station and looked around. Try as they might they could not find the hotel. They walked down the street and crossed over to the other side. Don was beginning to get a bit frustrated. He saw a security guard looking at them through the window. He tapped on the door and motioned to the guard. The guard came over and surprisingly unlocked the door. He asked if he could help. Don questioned him on the location of a hotel. Without a word he pointed to a large building across the street where they had just come from. There it was, as plain as day on the side of the building for all to see, the word "Hotel."

"We must be getting tired," Don thought as they retraced their steps back to the train station and then to the building next door. The entrance was almost obscure by North American standards. It was no wonder they had missed it. Once inside things were completely different. Several desk clerks in white shirts manned the front desk.

"We would like a room please," Don said.

"One night or two?" the clerk asked. Don thought he heard a slight trace of an Irish accent in his voice.

"One," he replied. As they filled out the register the desk clerk asked where they were from and where they were going.

"Ireland," Don said, "if we can figure out how." The clerk laughed.

"Don't bother with the trains," he said. "Just take the shuttle to the Stanstead Airport and get a Ryan Air flight to Shannon. That will be close to where you are going. I ought to know," he continued, "I come from there and it is the only way I go."

As they finished their business and went up to their room Don thought about the desk clerk's suggestion. He had their trip all planned in his mind, but now he was beginning to have second thoughts. He put it aside till morning. They had a short rest and then went down to the hotel restaurant for dinner. It was an expensive meal, but they didn't care. It had been a long day and a lot had happened. In fact it seemed more like a week than a day. Later that night as he lay in bed with Linda asleep beside him, Don reflected on the events of the past week. He realized it was just a week ago this day that he had met his Dolmetsch family in Buttenhausen. He thought back on the trip to Switzerland and the visit with cousin Mike. The trip to Sulz and the time spent with cousin Joachim Losch, then the tour with cousin Helga and her son Michele. He could scarcely believe it had only been a week. It seemed like at least a month, maybe even a year. As he rolled over in his sleep he breathed a prayer, thanking God for this marvellous experience. He was well aware this was more than happenstance. Far too much had come together in such an unbelievable fashion. It was as if he was being guided on his pilgrimage back to the land of his ancestors. He wondered if old Johann Adam Dolmetsch had asked God to reunite the family. He knew from the histories he had read that he was a God-fearing man so maybe that explained it all. He was still thinking about it as he drifted off into a deep, relaxing sleep.

They awoke about 8:30 the next morning. Don was surprised that they had slept that late. As he thought about it he realized that all the travelling and excitement must be starting to catch up with them. He decided to take it a bit easier this day and see if they could get back to feeling a bit more relaxed. They went to the restaurant for breakfast. The food was plentiful and the English style of eating was closer in breakfast fare to his own Canadian style breakfast. As he ate it though, he decided the Brits and the whole entire world had a long, long way to go before they could match a good Canadian breakfast. He smiled as he thought about it and about how horrified people would be should he choose to express his opinion. Still, it was absolutely true. In all his travels he had never been anywhere where they could match the typical Canadian style breakfast you could find in any Canadian restaurant or kitchen back home.

As they ate, they discussed their plans for the day. Don announced that he had decided to heed the desk clerk's advice and take a Ryan Air flight to Shannon, Ireland. Linda was shocked at first. This was not like Don. He did not particularly enjoy flying and disliked spending money even more.

She wondered how this would work out. They finished eating and returned to their room. They packed, checked out and headed for the Liverpool Station. The train for Stanstead Airport was easy to find and in no time they were on their way. At the airport they followed the other people to the main terminal building. This was an unusual airport and had only shorter flights to offer. He found the Ryan Air ticket counter and bought two tickets to the Shannon airport. The ticket clerk told him the flight was leaving in exactly one hour and fifteen minutes. He showed Don a large sign, high on the wall at the far end of the building.

"If you stand under that sign they will announce the boarding there and it will all work out," he told Don. Sure enough, it was exactly as the man had said. When it came close to the departure time they were led through a door and through the security check points into a large waiting area. The Ryan Air plane stood just outside the windows. In a very short time they were led down the stairs to the tarmac where they walked to the plane. Don and Linda sat down in the first seat behind the pilots' cabin. It was a good-sized plane and they had both flown on this type of aircraft before. Without any of the usual delays and nonsense so often found on international flights they were rolling down the runway and up in the air. It was not all that far to Ireland and the view was excellent on that particular day.

"Yes, it really is green," Don thought as they crossed the Irish coastline heading for the western side. It seemed to be only a few minutes before they touched down at the Shannon airport. Once inside Don found a tourist bureau and booked their lodging. He wanted to stay in a place called "The Willows" near Castle Matrix in Rathkeale. At first he had a bit of trouble as every request was met with a question or an opinion. Finally he became upset enough to express his displeasure (in no uncertain terms). When he explained that he wasn't doing a survey, he was only trying to book a room they seemed to understand the game had gone on long enough. Within minutes the booking was made and the deposit paid. Next they had to find transportation. That proved much harder. They found the bus stop but could find no schedule or no one who could explain which bus would take them to Rathkeale. Don was fed up at this point and recalled seeing a sign for a taxi inside the terminal. They made their way back and he asked the lady if they could hire a taxi to take them to Rathkeale.

"Certainly," the lady replied. "It will cost you forty pounds."

"Let's do it," Don said. Pounds or whatever it didn't matter to him now. He was within an hour's journey of completing his ancestor's journey from Germany to Rathkeale, Ireland. A little thing like money wasn't going to stand in his way now. As soon as they had a driver free, the lady beckoned them and they were on their way.

The taxi driver seemed at first an okay type, but as they soon found out his use of profanity was unrestrained. Don did not like this and Linda liked it even less. Don had worked around people all his life who spoke that way, but Canadian men, at least of Don's generation, had enough sense to not use it in mixed company. This man seemed to have no such inhibitions. He did however seem to pick up on the fact that it was not acceptable with his Canadian passengers and toned it down a bit. Finally they reached their destination. They unloaded their luggage and knocked on the door. There was no answer. Don knew they had a room reserved, so he decided they would go for a short walk and try the door later. He could see the old Castle Matrix through the trees. His brother Rae and his father had been there in the 1970s. He had seen pictures of it before. It was, according to the Irish tourist bureau, the first place potatoes were grown when Sir Walter Raleigh had returned with them from the New World. He knew this castle had once belonged to Lord Southwell. It was Lord Southwell who had been responsible for settling his ancestor and his family in this surrounding territory.

It was on that trip that Rae and his dad had met Hugh Delmage. Delmage was the latest Irish spelling of the old German name Dolmetsch. Don's spelling was the most prevalent in Canada and the USA, but all the same, they all knew that they were descendants of that one singular individual, Johann Adam Dolmetsch. Hugh had known a lot about the Canadian Dulmages and had even been to Canada as a young man. He had even shown Rae and his dad a doe-skin jacket he had bought on that trip almost fifty-five years before.

As they walked up to the corner and looked across at the castle, half hidden in the tall green trees, Don thought back on that trip his brother and father had made. He had not been very interested in all this genealogy stuff back then. He was curious about it, to be sure, but never envisioned himself coming to Ireland to see it for himself. He smiled to himself as he thought how his attitudes had changed.

After a bit they went back down the street to "The Willows" Bed and Breakfast. This time the door was answered. The lady was expecting them and showed them to their room. It was a very nice place and one could not complain about the price. As he signed in the lady told them that all of the houses on that street paid the Delmage estate for the right to live there. She said that she and her late husband had petitioned the Delmage estate and been granted a clear title by paying ten years of the normal fee in advance. As far as she knew, there were now no living members of the Delmage family around, but the estate was handled by the family's old law firm. Don asked about the old castle.

"Oh you must visit it," she said. "Just go up to the door and knock on it. Tell Liz who you are and she will let you in."

After stowing their luggage that is exactly what Linda and Don did. A horse and her colt watched them suspiciously as they made their way across the highway. Linda had the video camera going most of the time. She wanted this all on tape for sure. They had heard so much about this place and the role it played in the Dolmetsch family history.

It was exciting just to be here. They walked down the long overgrown lane. It was certainly a very old place. Don knew, beyond a shadow of a doubt, that his ancestor and his children had walked down this lane before. It was strange being here. Linda kept the camera going as Don knocked on the castle door. The door opened and five dogs made their way out into the sunlight.

"I'm Don Dulmage from Canada and my family used to live around here," Don said. He knew that Johann Adam Dolmetsch had not lived here, but Rae had told him of how it figured into the family history so he decided to go for it.

A teenage boy with very red hair had opened the door and now beckoned him in. As they signed the guest book Don noticed a very old harp sitting on a nearby table. Don told him of his ancestors' connection to this castle and the surrounding area. They seemed to have a hard time understanding that Don and Linda knew some of the history of this place and the influence it had on the Palatine settlers here.

After a cup of tea the young man Kieran took them on a tour of the old castle. It was everything one would expect. Evidence of bygone days and owners hung on the walls and on the mantles. Kieran took them all the way to the top of the castle where the view was absolutely beautiful. Don imagined for a moment that he was standing where old Johann Adam Dolmetsch and Lord Southwell would have been standing as they hammered out some deal between them. He had been told and had read that old Johann Adam and his descendants came with nothing, but in a very short time owned about half the land in this area. There were many places that appeared unchanged since the days when Don's family first came here. After the visit to the castle,

Don and Linda headed uptown to look for graveyards. The first one they came across was the old Church of Ireland graveyard on the main street. It was beginning to get a bit cloudy, but there was still enough light to see by, so they opened the gate and went in. Many of the stones were pointing at different angles. It seemed strange to see, as it was uncommon at home, but they reminded themselves these were very old gravestones. Many of the names were familiar to them from their family research. Some of the names were even from families of people they knew. There were Switzers and Sparlings everywhere. Don knew a couple of people who were actually Switzers back home and he had met one lady, who was the mother of one of his friends from church, who was born a Sparling before she married and changed her name. She had passed away a few months before, and the family seemed, to Don anyway, not to be that interested in the story of the Palatines so he decided not to take a picture of it. He knew it was the exact right family, but did not know how to spark their interest. He wasn't sure if it was because "he" had told them about the family history or if they were just not interested. Whatever the case, it puzzled him.

As they walked through the graveyard they saw three young boys come around the corner, by the fuel tank, at the back of the church. The leader spotted Don and Linda and without a moment's hesitation asked who they were.

"I'm Don Dulmage from Canada," said Don.

"Well I'd be Adam Teskey from Ireland," the young leader said.

"Teskey?" said Don. "I saw in the old family history that two Teskeys married two Dulmages. Once in Germany before coming here and once after they were here."

"Well then," the young lad said, "that would make us cousins so I'll be coming up there to shake your hand."

Don couldn't help but smile at this eleven-year-old who spoke like he was going on forty. Soon they were on a guided tour of the graveyard accompanied by all the stories that young boys have to tell about such things. What surprised Don was that Adam seemed to know a lot about the Palatine families. Adam would go to one particular grave and say to Don, "now Don, I'd be thinking this would be one of your people." Every time Don would read the stone and realize Adam was right. That particular family had married into the Dulmage line. Linda had a great time watching Don and Adam, with Adam's friends trailing silently along behind. It was obvious that despite their difference in age Adam and Don were getting along just fine.

Here young Adam Teskey gives Don and Linda a tour of the old original sights around Rathekeale, Ireland, where both his (Teskey) and Don's (Dolmetsch) ancestors first settled. A better guide for the area you would not find!

"Are there any Dulmage graves here?" Don asked.

"Not here, that I know of," Adam said, "but there are lots of Delmage graves around (referring to the Irish spelling and slightly different way of pronouncing the name). He called over his friend. "Go tell my mother where I'm at," he said, "and tell her I'm here with a Delmage from Canada."

Don watched in amazement as Adam's friend obeyed without a word. It was obvious this young fellow was a natural born leader.

"We'll be hearing about him someday," Don thought. Don had met a lot of people in his life both young and old but few had the qualities he saw in this young man. As they left the graveyard Adam turned to Don and asked, "now Don, would you be wanting to know how Annie Delmage died?"

"Sure," said Don.

"Well," said Adam, "She was sitting by the fire, you know, and a flame jumped out and licked her arm. She run all the way to Austin Bovenizer's house and they took her to the hospital but she was too far gone and she slipped away in the night." Despite the colourfulness of Adam's rendition, Don was to find out the next day that it was an absolutely accurate account of the death of the last living member of his direct family in Rathkeale. It bothered him that this relative (even though he had never met her) had come to such an untimely end. He would think about it from time to time in the year to come as he pondered his experiences in Ireland.

Before he could respond the back door, of a building leading to the churchyard, opened and a woman stepped out with Adam's friend right behind her. Don realized this must be Adam's mother. He introduced himself and Linda. She introduced herself as Adam's mother and invited them inside the building. Once inside they realized it was actually the school. She told them she was the schoolteacher and showed them around. Linda was pleased by this as she had taught primary grades in Canada for thirty-five years. They immediately hit it off as she showed Linda and Don around the school. On one side was a cardboard display the students had made in memory of the Palatine families who had come to this area from Germany in 1709. Mock tombstones were on the display with the names "Miller, Switzer, Sparling, Teskey, Delmage and Heck. Now Don understood why Adam seemed to understand what they were looking for. He had been studying it in school. Adam showed Don the school's computer and even took a look at Don's web site. He told Don he had e-mail but did not get much mail. As they left the school Adam's mother asked Don and Linda where they were going.

"We thought about going to the Rathkeale House for supper," Don said. "Is it any good?"

"Oh, you'll like that," she replied. "Come with me. I will drive you there."

"Thanks," Don replied as they piled into the car. When they arrived at the Rathkeale House Adam asked Don if he would e-mail him when he got home.

"Sure," Don told him. "What is your e-mail?" Adam said it slowly to make sure Don understood. "Have you got that now?" he asked. Don nodded.

"You had better repeat it just to be sure," Adam said, obviously parroting something he had heard from his mother. Don couldn't help but smile at his newfound friend but obliged him by repeating the e-mail he had just been given. With that Adam opened the door and got out so Don could exit the vehicle. They shook hands and then Don and

Linda walked up to the Rathkeale House as the Teskey car drove away.

Dinner was good and the service was excellent. The food, while tasty, was quite different to what Don and Linda were used to. All part of the Irish experience Don thought as he cleaned his plate. He had already forgotten what it was called but it was very good just the same.

After supper they walked by the other two churches in town and then up the old path to where "The Willows" Bed and Breakfast lay. On the way they passed a small creek.

"I bet that would be good for fishing," Don thought thinking back on his boyhood days when he went fishing everyday after school.

"I wonder if any of my ancestors ever tried fishing here?" he thought. By now "The Willows" was in sight and they quickened their pace as they could see their goal. Once in their room they were in bed and asleep within minutes. It had been another long, eventful day.

The next morning they arose and got ready for the day. A good hearty breakfast awaited them and they made the most of it. The owner of the bed and breakfast had phoned Mr. Austin Bovenizer, who looked after the Irish Palatine Heritage Centre, just a few minutes walk from "The Willows" and had arranged for Don and Linda to meet him there at 11:00 am. Don wanted to see the old Heck-Embury Church while they were here and asked about the possibility of getting a taxi to run them out and back to the church before their 11:00 am museum appointment. The lady explained where and how to get a taxi and acknowledged it should work out just fine. Even though they were booked for only one night she told them they could leave their luggage there while they went exploring. They finished breakfast and set out to find the taxi stand. At the taxi stand was a coin-operated phone one used to order a taxi. Don went through about five pounds in change with no results. He looked for someone to ask but could find no one. They walked back up the street until they found an open grocery store. Don went in and asked how one got a taxi. Nobody seemed to know. Time was running out and so was Don's patience.

"That does it!" he said. "I am going to walk." With that he set off down the street. Linda was following along behind. Surely he was not serious.

"Do you know how far it is?" she asked. He pointed to the sign on the corner without slowing down. It read "Heck-Embury Church twelve miles."

"It's twelve miles," he said and kept on walking.

"How will we get back in time for the museum if we do find it?" Linda asked.

"I have a plan," Don said.

"Can I hear it?" came the reply. "Yup." he said. "If we split the time in two and give ourselves a five minute cushion we can walk for one hour and twenty minutes before we have to turn around to be back on time. If we don't find it by then we will have to forget it, but I didn't come 3000 miles to miss going there!"

"Don Dulmage, you're an incredibly stubborn man!" Linda said. Don pretended he didn't hear her. This was hardly a news flash. He had been told that many times before in his fifty-one years. Linda was unsure of his plan, but followed along. From his pace she could tell he was serious, but it was not easy walking. The road was narrow with almost no shoulder and at this time of day the traffic was heavy. They walked for about an hour. Finally they saw a new sign indicating they had to take a side road.

There were few houses now and it was a more rural setting. The sideroad proved to be short and they found themselves back on a paved road again. Don kept looking at his watch. Linda knew time was short, but also knew better than to ask. Don never let up as he walked ahead. Suddenly Linda saw it off to the right. Don was already halfway by it but there it was, the old Heck-Embury Church. She called to Don and pointed to the sign. Relief flooded his face as he turned around and headed into the churchyard. They had only a few minutes to look around but at least they had made it there. They searched the graveyard. Like before they found many of the names they knew from their family research, but only one direct relative, a "Delmege" man from the 1800s with the newest Irish spelling of that old German name. They took as much time as they dared and took several photos before they began the long trek back to the museum. They arrived with just minutes to spare and before they could even catch their breath a silver-grey car pulled into the yard. A tall man about Don's age got out and introduced himself. It was the actual Mr. Austin Bovenizer they had heard so much about, both from Adam Teskey and from their hostess at the bed and break-fast. As Austin opened the museum he asked about their trip. Don told him of meeting the original Dolmetsch family in Germany. He told how they had been to Switzerland, Holland and England before coming here. Austin seemed somewhat surprised, but went on to show them around the museum. There was a lot of Dolmetsch/Delmage things on display including a couple of letters written by Don's original ancestors. One was the actual letter while another was a copy. Austin told them the museum had recently received these from an estate settlement and that there were many original Dolmetsch family letters. He was unable to say which ones for sure, but told them they had all been photographed for microfiche display. The museum was expecting to have a system for printing from these microfiche copies in the near future and he might be able to provide Don with copies of the letters written by the people he had just asked about. In return Austin asked Don if he would write a synopsis of the story of his adventure and send it to him by e-mail. Used to writing his own highly opinionated newspaper column as well as having written numerous magazine articles, Don knew he could deliver on his promise. Austin gave them a good tour of the museum and took time to answer any questions they asked. As they were leaving he also told Don that his own grandmother was a Delmege.

"More cousins," Don thought. "This trip was becoming very unbelievable." They took time for a photo, then shook hands and parted company. After a short walk to "The Willows" Don and Linda sat down to talk with their hostess.

"I couldn't find a taxi this morning," Don said.

"Oh no, " she replied. "They only run here after 6:00 pm. The men that run them at night are working during the day." Don said nothing. He was dumbfounded. Somewhere, that very morning when they were asking about taking a taxi to the Heck-Embury Church they must have gotten their wires crossed. He was sure he had understood correctly but now was beginning to doubt himself. Graciously the lady offered to drive them to the bus stop to save them the walk. Don and Linda were both grateful for the offer. They were both beginning to stiffen up from that morning's marathon walk. The bus was a long time coming. The locals eyed them suspiciously and kept moving away as they waited for the bus. Once onboard they watched Rathkeale and the surrounding area disappear from view. It was good to have been there and they were glad they had come. Don wondered if they would ever get a chance to return.

A few days later, back home in Canada, Don thought back over the great adventure of the last few weeks. He had just e-mailed Austin Bovenizer that morning to see exactly what type of article he had in mind for Don to write. Austin had been very specific and so Don was already typing away. By the next morning he had it proofread and sent it on its way.

Don sat back in his chair and reflected on the trip.It was hard to believe all that had happened. Everything they had wanted to see relating to the Dolmetsch family they had seen. On top of that they had discovered things and met people they never even knew existed. It had been a very exciting time. Even now Don had to pinch himself as he thought about it. "There must be more to this than we realize. Too much of the unusual has happened. It must be part of God's plan. Maybe this is the job I was born for. Maybe I am just fulfilling a request old Johann Adam Dolmetsch made of God many years ago? I wonder?" He grew sleepy as he sat there thinking about it. Eventually he shut the computer down and headed off to bed. This had truly been "The Great Adventure." With that thought in his head and a smile on his face he drifted off into deep relaxing sleep.

Austin turned on his computer and saw Don's name come up again on his e-mail screen. As he clicked on it he saw the attached article. That was faster than he expected and he was a bit taken aback. He printed it out and took a few minutes to read it before quitting for the day. Everything he had asked for was there. He typed a short letter of thanks to Don and then sent it on its way. As he reread the story this is what he read.

Chapter 9

The Great Adventure

The first time I remember having any serious thoughts about my heritage was when I was having dinner with my friends, the Nighswander family, in Altona, Ontario. We had recently moved to the area and these were some of my first visits out in the community. We were sitting at the table when the father, Joe Nighswander asked me "Now Don, what type of a name is Dulmage?"

"It's a German name," I answered, not quite knowing why, but I remembered my father telling me that. "Are you sure?" Joe asked, "Yup," I answered as I stuffed down another chocolate brownie. "Can you say Albert Schweizter?" he asked. "Sure," I said, "Albert SchVeitzer." "Well," he replied cautiously, "maybe—not too many English speaking people can say it properly."

It was from that moment on that I carried an unrelenting curiosity of who we actually were and where we came from. The Nighswanders, who are Mennonites, knew a great deal of their family history. Even at the tender age of six or seven it didn't seem right that mine should remain a mystery.

I knew my mom's mother was of German descent because she had taught us to count to ten in German and I had even heard her speak it at the Kitchener farmer's market. Mom knew a bit of German and taught us two or three phrases, but that was all. I didn't take advantage of the opportunities that were around me as Joe Nighswander's brother, Fred, lived across the road and that household often spoke Pennsylvania Deutsch around the farm. While not the exact dialect I would need it would certainly have given me a boost in learning the language, but I never bothered.

Many years later, after I was married (1970) my dad showed me a first edition copy of a book called "To Their Heirs Forever" written by Eula Lapp. This book had a wealth of information I had not seen before and it reawakened my interest in who I was. I learned from that book that our original name was Dolmetsch and that we were definitely from Germany by way of Ireland. The first edition of this book was hard for me to follow, but I never forgot it. Years later I obtained the final edition in hard cover. It was a beautiful book and could be read like a story. I followed my ancestor's route down the Rhine to Rotterdam, Holland. I saw the name of the ship (the Bachelor) that he had sailed to England on. I saw his entry as Johann Adam Dolmetsch, thirty years old, husbandman and vine-dresser. It listed his wife and children who came with him. It told of his stay in the Blackheath refugee camp and of his placement in Rathkeale, Ireland. It told how the family flourished and of his passing at Castle Matrix in 1751. I ate this information up and stored it away. About this time my dad and my youngest brother, Rae, went to Ireland on a vacation and visited many of the Dolmetsch family sites around that area. They came back with a great deal of information and a large number of pictures. While there they met with Hugh Delmage as well as his wife and daughter. Hugh had been to Canada around the turn of the last century (1900) and seemed to know a lot more about us than we did about him.

Another thing I learned from that book was that Jacob Dolmage (as he spelled it) left Ireland for America aboard the ship Pery in 1760. These were verifiable records, so there was no doubt. With him were his wife and two sons, Jacob and David. His oldest son, John, had sailed for America three years earlier as a soldier of the British Crown. They first had lived in what is now New York City but later moved to Duane's Patent near Cambridge, New York. John, Jacob Jr. and David all used the spelling Dulmage for their last name.

During the American Revolution John and David fought for the British side, I am sure, out of loyalty to the country who had befriended their great-grandfather Johann Adam Dolmetsch. Jacob Dolmage senior and his wife were past the age of participating in this disagreement and petitioned the governor for permission to go to New York. It was granted and Jacob senior and his wife stayed on in New York. They both are recorded as having passed away near Albany, New York. As the war drew to a close, those who had been loyal to the British Crown lost what they had and were sent to what is now Canada. Among them were David and John Dulmage and their families. It is unclear what became of Jacob Dulmage Jr. Some say he went to New Jersey before the Revolution started but I do not know for sure. Many of these "Loyalists," as we now refer to them, were sent to Sorel, Quebec, while they awaited land grants for their military service from the British Crown. David Dulmage and family were among those there and it was while here that his son David Jr. was born. David Dulmage and family eventually received grants in what is now known as Prince Edward County, Ontario, Canada and settled there, in the southern part.

The Dulmages can still be found in Prince Edward County today as that is where I live and where my father and his forefathers, right back to David Jr.'s sons, were born.

The year 1984 marked the bicentennial of the great Loyalist settlement in this area and in honour of that my wife Linda and I took a trip to New York state in the Cambridge area to see if we could find where my family used to live. It took little effort to find the old road winding across the bridge and up the hills to the places where they used to farm. I was not able to find the Dulmage places exactly but evidence of their neighbours and close relatives (by marriage), the Emburys and Switzers were abundant. Even the Old Red Grocery still exists at the end of the road as it did in the 1700s.

As we drove further along the Old Tory Road we passed an old cemetery that was full of Peck gravestones. Peck is my wife's maiden name and we surmised that these Dulmages and Pecks had likely know each other back then as it was a very short distance between the two locations. These spots are located on the New York/Vermont border in the area where Ethan Allen and his Green Mountain Boys were active during the American Revolution. I was able to find some veiled references to those five Tory families in the hills in some of his writings and I now knew exactly whom he was referring to: the Hecks, Emburys, Millers, Switzers and Dulmages. I wished I had known this while studying history in school. I would probably have been a much better student. We spent quite a bit of time around there and saw the old Philip Embury Church as well as many other sites mentioned in "To Their Heirs Forever." On the way home we stopped at Prescott and visited the Blue Church where Barbara Heck is memorialized for her work as an early Methodist.

Over the next few years we visited as many sites as possible that we could find related to my Dulmage family. Among those were the cemetery at South Bay and the cemetery in Cherry Valley both of which are right here in our beloved Prince Edward County. There were many gravestones. Some were from my direct line of David Dulmage Jr. and some from his brothers and sisters. I found this all very interesting but it had still not satisfied my thirst for knowledge of my family's German roots. It was during this time I started trying to learn German. I bought a German Bible with a parallel King James English translation. It took me three years to read it through. While I find it a very worthwhile book to read it did not help me very much with my German. I am sure it laid a foundation, of course, but I still could not speak it or read it with any comprehension. I think having the English nearby was a big hindrance. I think the best way to learn a language is by immersion. After all, that is how I learned to speak English when I was a baby.

As the year 2000 approached my wife mentioned that she wanted to go to Oberammergau for the millennium year. I welcomed the idea as I thought I might at least be able to see the land my ancestors came from. We left Toronto, Canada on May 27, 2001. We had purchased a German rail-pass for each of us and were prepared to explore. After landing in Frankfurt we boarded the train for Karlsruhe and transferred to the train for Pforzheim. That was the last place the book said that Johann Adam Dolmetsch is recorded being before leaving Germany by boat for Rotterdam.

It was a thrill for me as we stepped from the train into the town where I knew, for sure, my ancestor had been. It is a beautiful place as well and I enjoyed staying there. About a month before I left home I had been in touch with Reta Selleck of North Carolina. Reta was also a Dolmetsch descendant. Her ancestor was John Dulmage of Prince Edward County who just happens to be the son of David Dulmage who is also my direct ancestor. Reta has compiled a tremendous amount of information on the Dulmage (and Roblin) families. She sent me all she had on Johann Adam Dolmetsch as to where he had lived and worked. I had this additional information tucked in the front of my suitcase just in case I had the chance to visit any of those areas. My first real break came the next morning. As with many of us interested in our family's heritage, I often check the phone book in every town where I stay just in case there are some family members there. Here in Pforzheim there were no phone books in the room. As I paid the hotel bill I asked to see a phone book. "Something I could look up for you sir?" the clerk asked. I hesitated for a couple of seconds. I had read and had been told many times there are no more members of the Dolmetsch family left in Germany. The trouble was I had learned in the later years of my life to seize opportunity when it presents itself. I had nothing to lose so I said "I would like to see if any of my ancestor's descendants still live here. This is the last place in Germany he was recorded as having been before leaving." He began to search through the book. "It is not spelled like my name is," I said (I knew he was using my credit card name to identify me.) "It is spelled Do—" He held up his hand and interrupted me. "I know, Sir," he said in a very definite tone. You could have knocked me over with a feather. I guess he could tell from the anglicized spelling and my pronunciation just how it would be in German. He handed me the book with his finger on two names. "There are two here, Sir" he said, "But they have double Ls."

My heart leapt inside me. This wasn't supposed to be. I knew from info Reta had sent me (that I believe came from a translation of the old Dolmetsch family book by JAB Dulmage of the Ottawa Valley area) that Dollmetsch was a branch of the family that developed for some reason around the 1500s. I wasn't prepared for this. I only knew about fifty words in German and I am a very shy individual. I wrote the information down on the sheet of paper he had provided and went on my way. "I will deal with this when I get home." I thought. "That was almost too easy."

While in Germany we visited many of the places that I had learned from books and from the information Reta Selleck had shared with me. My favourite was the visit to Alzey where I knew for sure Johann Adam Dolmetsch had been. In fact, some of his family records (births and deaths) have been found there in that town. Freimersheim, where he had actually lived, proved too difficult to get to for this trip but we visited all the places we could that were accessible by railway.

After we came home I began to search in earnest. I con- tacted a ham radio operator by e-mail to see if there were any hams in Germany with the name Dolmetsch.(I myself am a ham, VE3LYX.) He said "no" but there were several names in the phone book. I had to ask him this question in German as he did not quite understand what I had asked in English. I used a small German/English phrase book we had bought for our trip to Germany to phrase the question. He seemed pleased because he said "Nicht schlecht" (not bad) when he answered me. I began to search for a way to look into the European phone book. One night, quite by accident, I stumbled onto it and immediately entered the name Dolmetsch. I printed out the search results immediately. (This is very, very important when researching because sometimes it is very hard or impossible to find the same information later on. Always print everything you find. You won't be sorry.) Many of the listings were translation services as that is what the name Dolmetsch means. That much I had known for many years. I sorted through the listings until I had all the private homes. I drafted a letter and sent it to every address. It stated who I was, who my ancestor was and that I wanted to meet at least one of the original family, which, of course, they must be. I waited for weeks. I received three letters back unopened and one indignant reply. That man had someone write it for him in English. It stated that there was no way we were relatives and he sent a chart of the Dolmetsch family to prove it. I noticed immediately that the chart contained a reference that I and many others had been missing. It was #55B Joseph, who is believed by several researchers to be, most likely, Johann Adam Dolmetsch's father. (That piece of research is a whole other story.)

A couple of weeks later I received an e-mail from a Karin Dolmetsch. She had e-mailed me from the e-mail address I had stamped on my letter. She told in the letter how her family had gotten together with my letters that they all had received. She explained that, for many of them, English was not a language they spoke. She had been elected to answer me because she spoke it very well. She sent greetings from the family and gave me a brief description of who they were and their current occupations. She also told me her dad would like to meet me at a family picnic, June 3, 2001. I could hardly believe my eyes. This was more than I had ever hoped for.

Over the next few weeks she would occasionally e-mail me with more information. Her father also sent a package containing a copy of an old family history called "Der Stammfolge der Familie Dolmetsch" (the genealogy of the family Dolmetsch). I had heard of this book from some of JAB Dulmage's research but had been told from his notes that it was now nonexistent except for a water damaged copy he had seen and had hired someone to partially translate. Here was my own private copy in the original Deutsch. I used a software program and a German/English dictionary to translate it. It was very interesting. They also sent me pictures of their immediate family. I was amazed to see that there were strong family resemblances, even after all these years. In one picture her brother, Marc Dolmetsch, then in his late teens or early twenties bore a striking resemblance to my nephew, David Dulmage. David also has a younger brother, Mark Dulmage, and it will be interesting to see what he looks like when he grows older. I scanned in several family photos and sent them to the family in Germany. After a lot of e-mails and letters exchanged hands I realized that Karin was trying to finish university, find an apartment and find a suitable job, all the while she was acting as the family go between. I wanted to get her something for her efforts. We had located a pen and ink sketch done by a local artist of the False Ducks Lighthouse here in Prince Edward County. That lighthouse had, for a time, been manned by the Dulmage family (Dorland Dulmage) and so I got a bit of that history as well. My wife and I took it to Mailboxes Unlimited where they packaged it and sent it to Karin's address at university. It was just an attempt, in some small way, to thank her for all she had done for us. I tracked the package and knew it had been delivered but I had not had a reply. About this time I had sold a copy of an automotive book I had written to a Mike Schwienbacher in Germany. Actually I donated it to him in honour of my German ancestors as he was the first from Germany to order one. He had e-mailed me occasionally and one day asked me if I knew that my name in German (Dulmage) was spelled Dolmetsch. He went on to say that he had checked the phone records and there were about sixteen Dolmetsches in Germany. I replied that I knew this already and related the above story, as well as my concerns about the package actually making its way to Karin Dolmetsch's hands. I was afraid it had gotten to her apartment, but that by that time she had already moved. He offered to phone the family and check so I gave him her father's name (he already had the phone numbers). He said that wasn't too far and he would call the next day. The next morning he e-mailed that he had talked to the Dolmetsch family for quite a while. "They are very friendly people," he said, "but they don't speak English. I will teach you German by e-mail." I wondered how that would work but agreed to give it a try. At first it was very difficult. I went through several dictionaries until I finally found one that would work for me (Bantam New College

German English Dictionary by John C Traupman PhD).
Finally, I was able to try to write a bit in German. It seemed
impossible at first, but I could almost hear old Johann
Adam Dolmetsch whispering in my ear "Go on son, you
can do this!" This whole project seemed to me to be what I
had been born for. It seemed to me I was assigned this job
from "above." I pressed on with e-mails in German
everyday. Soon Mike's mother, Renate Schwienbacher,
joined in and began e-mailing me in German every morning.
More and more I could make out what was being said. I
borrowed newspapers from German-speaking friends as
well as language books. I bought software programs to help
me learn the vocabulary and structure. I bought audio tapes
and played them in my truck whenever I drove to help get
my ear accustomed to the sound of the language. I also listened to Deutsche Welle Radio from Germany on my short-
wave set for about an hour every night. I soon realized the
language was vast and I probably would never learn it all so
I concentrated on learning what I would need in the immediate future. I must say, that having tried all of the above,
the e-mail method is by far the fastest and best way I have
ever seen to pick up a language. I have also watched Renate
Schwienbacher go from almost no English to a comprehen-
sible level with the language in about six weeks. I have since
worked with others with similar results. As time progressed,
I became fairly comfortable in the language and stopped
translating but just absorbed it. I am not even remotely
close to fluent, even now, but I understand and speak
enough to communicate. Time seemed to fly. We received a
confirmation on our attendance at the family picnic from
Karin and she made arrangements of where and how she
would meet us in Germany. Before we knew it we were on

a plane and at the Schwienbacher's home in Germany. By now we had become quite good friends. They fed us and took care of us while we were there. Mike and his girlfriend, Noiy, drove us to Freimersheim, Framersheim and Alzey where Johann Adam Dolmetsch had lived and worked. We strolled around the streets and looked in the churches where we knew they had actually been. I cannot thank him and his family enough for the help and care they provided. On Sunday morning Mike and Noiy packed our suitcases in the trunk of their car and drove us to the meeting place. Karin had told me to phone her cell phone number when I got close so I dialed it as we drew near to the spot. She answered immediately "Karin Dull-Maytch" I was shocked to hear that they pronounced the name just like we do in Canada. I panicked a bit but Mike took the phone and stepped out of the car to get the final instructions. Eventually we got to a well-known spot in the town where they lived. He called Karin again and told her exactly where we were. It had begun to rain but I didn't care. He looked over at me and grinned "It is hard for you, this part. Yes?" "Yes," I said. This all seemed so impossible. Within a few minutes an older immaculate 69 Mercedes hardtop drove up followed closely behind by a black Volkswagen. I could see Karin in the driver's seat of the VW smiling but she waited till the man got out of the Mercedes before she stepped out. The door of the Mercedes opened and Marc Dolmetsch got out and walked to the back of the car where I was standing. "Marc Dolmetsch, I presume" I said. "Hi, I'm Don" He grinned and shook my hand. Mike Schwienbacher snapped a photo at the very second we shook hands. It couldn't have been more perfect. Karin was out of her car by now and she came over and we gave each other a big hug. Without her help and patience this moment would never have happened. After introductions all around, Marc asked Mike and Noiy to follow us to the family party. Marc spoke perfect English as he had worked for a time in England. We discussed so many family things during the drive that I am hard pressed to remember them. I still had to pinch myself from time to time to be sure I wasn't dreaming. Soon we were at the house and were introduced all around. These people really were very similar to my immediate family and I felt right at home. A few of the younger members of the family could speak English but most of the conversation was in German. I was able to understand most of what was going on and I knew how to ask for clarification. If things got real bad Martin would call Karin over to help us both out. We used whatever words worked. Several others who knew English, even just a bit, stuck around to help in the tough places. Actually it went very well. I liked these people very much. They were just like what they actually are, "family." As we sat there talking one of the most unusual things happened that went beyond what anyone would have dreamed. Albrecht Dolmetsch was sitting with Martin and me along with one of the sons. As we talked he was leafing through an old photo book of the Dolmetsch men. The book went back as far in time as to when photography first became available. It was quite thick. Suddenly I felt him tugging my shirt sleeve. "Don, Don, that is you!" he said excitedly in German. When I looked, I saw a picture of one of the Dolmetsch ancestors that was almost the exact likeness of me. Did I locate the right branch of the family? Were these really my relatives? Look at the accompanying photos of me and the one from the old Dolmetsch photo book and you be the judge. For me, and for them, any questions we might have had vanished at that moment and I knew that we truly were "back home."

Photo of Don Dulmage   *Photo from old Dolmetsch
                                        family album.*

The rest of the trip went equally well. We were able to meet with a Swiss Dolmetsch cousin who is from the same family branch as Martin Dolmetsch. This cousin found me by way of my web site just a few days after I received the first e-mail from Karin Dolmetsch. There was no correspondence between the two family branches. That is just how it happened, strange as that may seem. We were able to visit some archives and see original family birth entries of my actual line from the 1600s. We met with another branch of the family in Asperg and discovered they knew all the history right back to the 1400s. They showed us places the family had lived and gave us several books on the specific towns where Dolmetsch people were prominent. We have been able to remain in contact and those e-mails and letters are something I really enjoy. To complete our trip we sailed down the Rhine to Holland then took a ship across to England. From there we went to Ireland, arriving in Limerick and spending the night in Rathkeale, which is the area where my ancestor Johann Adam Dolmetsch settled and was buried (1751). We visited the fine Palatine Heritage Centre and got a chance to spend some time with Austin Bovenizer who is in charge of the museum there. By now we had traced Johann Adam Dolmetsch's journey from where it is believed he was born to where we know he actually died. A few days later we were back in another stronghold of Dolmetsch or rather Dulmage (as we spell it) family history, Prince Edward County, Ontario, Canada. Home to me! Four-hundred photos and four videotapes later I am still as thrilled as when I was there. It truly was "The Great Adventure" or as Martin Dolmetsch so aptly put it "Der Grossartig Abenteuer."

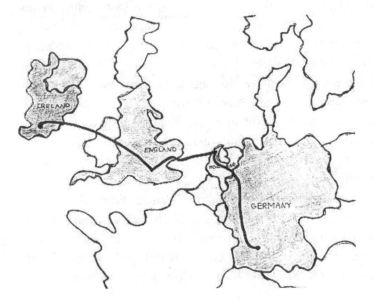

This map shows the original journey of Johann Adam Dolmetsch, from his birthplace (Sulz, Germany, 1678) to his burial place (Rathekeale, Ireland, 1751) and is the same route taken by his grandson, Don Dulmage, some 292 years later, retracing his ancestor's footsteps.

Postscript

As you might imagine, this experience has had a profound effect on my life. Possibly, because things like this don't happen to me. Almost from the moment this adventure began until it ended everything clicked or came together in an unbelievable way. It had never been so before and may never be again. To have had this experience at all fills me with gratitude and not a day goes by that I don't think about it. I also learned some things about myself.

During my moments of frustration, some of which I am not particularly proud of, I learned, after some reflection, that I have trouble dealing with certain types of people who come from certain areas of the world. Strange as it may seem, I had never made the connection before. I have come to believe that the way each of us thinks and reasons is tied in more with our ethnic background than I ever would have previously thought. To be certain, our upbringing plays an important role but, I believe more now than ever, our ethnic background also has a major influence. This has helped me with my interpersonal relationships and given me a new sense of tolerance and understanding for differing points of view. More often than not, we come to the same conclusion in the end but we often take very different routes to get there. I realize in this age of "political correctness" this view may not be popular, however it does appear to me, nevertheless, to be true.

Another thing I learned is to own your own project. Never quit looking until you have satisfied yourself that it is a dead end. Throw out no information just because someone has suggested it or because it doesn't "for the moment" appear to fit. Many times I felt or was told I had gone down the wrong path only to find out the paths rejoined later on. I was glad I had saved what I had been tempted to discard.

I also learned to share information. Whenever I found someone willing to share with me I made it a rule to share freely with him. Some were very generous and some were less than forthcoming. I am afraid I must confess that those in the latter category may have quickly found themselves outside the loop. I have developed a strong distaste for the takers of this world who want help but have no intention of sharing with others.

Reta Selleck was one who helped me a great deal. She shared what she had compiled freely and it was of tremendous help to me. There is little she could ask for that I would not gladly give.

Michele Solimando is another who has spent countless hours searching, compiling and communicating with others. Without his help this story would be only half here. His knowledge of the early Dolmetsch family history has no equal in my opinion and besides he is a real fun guy to be around.

His mother, Helga, has proven to be a worthy relative as well. True to her word she has kept up e-mail communication with us for almost a year. As she suggested, she writes me in German and I reply in English. I hope this continues for many years.

Martin Dolmetsch deserves a great deal of credit as well. He took a chance on inviting this strange Canadian to his home in Germany. Someone he had never heard of or seen before. In fact, someone who didn't even spell the family name the same. I am sure it was not easy having someone who could barely speak the language invade his family gathering, but he, for some reason, took that chance. Had he not done so there would be no story to write.

For his daughter, Karin, who was our "go-between" I have a special place in my heart. By the time we got there I felt I knew her quite well. I wish her a long and happy life. Thank you Karin.

Mike Dolmetsch, who held up the Swiss end of things, shared freely without hesitation. I hope someday to see him again.

Joachim Losch, who was with us in Sulz, was a big help. I hope he has a long and happy retirement.

And last, but not least, there is the family Schwienbacher of Bruchkoebel, Germany. They have helped us immeasurably, as friends, as language instructors, as chauffeurs, as well as providing us with a homebase from which to set out, what can I say? Words do not come easy to describe the great help they have been. May all their dreams come true.

Since we have returned home we have met approximately one new relative per week. Some in person and some by computer. I do not understand this phenomenon but am truly thankful for it.

What the future holds, I do not know. It is my desire to see some of my German Dolmetsch family relatives come to Canada for a visit and to see how the other half (literally) of this old family lives. That would make me very happy.

I am back home now, adjusting to a relatively normal life with its ups and downs. It is hard for me to believe that all of the things in this book actually took place, but they did. I often wonder what life would be like if I hadn't pursued this but it really doesn't matter now. It seemed to me, at the time, that I really had no choice. It was, to me, for the lack of a better word, my destiny, my assignment, and I carried it out to the best of my ability. That suits me just fine, too. I wouldn't have missed this for anything.

—*Donald Karl Dulmage.*